LEADING LIFE TO THE FULL

SCRIPTURAL REFLECTIONS ON LEADERSHIP IN CATHOLIC SCHOOLS

David Tuohy SJ

First published 2005 by
Veritas Publications
7/8 Lower Abbey Street
Dublin 1
Ireland
Email publications@veritas.ie
Website www.veritas.ie

ISBN 1 85390 872 X

Printed in the Republic of Ireland
by Betaprint Ltd.

Veritas books are printed on paper made from the wood pulp of
managed forests. For every tree felled, at least one tree is planted,
thereby renewing natural resources.

To the memory of my mother, Peg

CONTENTS

INTRODUCTION

The context of leadership in Catholic schools

The past twenty years have seen a major change in the governance landscape of Irish education. In the voluntary secondary school sector, the profile of personnel in schools has become predominantly lay. A brief look at the personnel figures, as illustrated in Table 1 shows the rapid increase in the number of teachers in this sector of second-level education, as well as the declining number of religious. Although a number of religious are also involved in schools on a part-time basis, they are not in receipt of a salary from the Department of Education and Science. However, this number is also declining and does not make a significant difference to the overall picture.

Table 1. The number of lay and religious teachers in voluntary secondary schools and community schools on incremental salaries in selected years.

	Lay	Religious	Religious as % of total
1965-66	2,220	2,033	48%
1975-76	8,354	2,452	23%
1985-86	12,407	1,877	13%
1999	n/a	633	6%

(Source: *Department of Education: Tuarascail Staitistiuil;* Dail Debates. Written Answer 19/12/91 cols. 2601: Breen M.J. (ed) *A Fire in the Forest,* Dublin, Veritas, 2001)

Initially, the religious congregations maintained a high profile in running their schools, reserving the key administrative roles of principal and chairperson of boards of management for a member of the congregation. A combination of factors led to a re-evaluation of that strategy. Declining numbers and an ageing profile in the religious congregations, allied with a developing commitment to participative democracy, has given rise to a new situation where the majority of schools under the trusteeship of religious congregations now have lay principals. Some congregations are in the process of setting up new forms of trusteeship for their schools. For some, this will mean the exercise of collaborative or joint trusteeship with other congregations. For others, trusteeship will be handed over to lay trustees, who will assume responsibility for the legal aspects of the schools and their Catholic ethos.

Primary education has traditionally been organised on a parish basis under the patronage of the bishop. The local clergy still play a strong managerial role. However, lay principals have traditionally exercised the professional leadership roles. Frequently, clergy and teachers have forged a strong partnership in the faith development of young people, especially centred on initiation rites of First Communion and Confirmation. In recent years, we have seen the development of a more participative and democratic process in the governance of these schools, with the introduction of equal representation of patrons, parents and teachers on boards of management.

With the increasing complexity of school management, a new interest has developed in training individuals for the leadership role of principal. Pre-service courses aim to develop technical and leadership skills in individuals who aspire to leadership positions, either as principals or at middle-management level. In-service courses also give support to those who are in position as leaders. These courses are built around technical skills such as finance, timetabling, personnel, planning and implementation. They include aspects of educational leadership such as legal responsibilities, curriculum development, instructional leadership, staff development and motivation, strategic planning and vision setting. Very little attention has, as yet, been paid to the specific Christian and Catholic element of school vision. There has been an assumption that leaders will be found who are sympathetic to and committed to developing a Christian ethos in the schools. To a large extent, this assumption has been well-founded and the first generation of lay principals have been very committed to maintaining the ethos they inherited.

However, these principals meet challenges not met by their religious predecessors. The context of Irish society, with a more secular value system, is very different from that of fifty, even twenty years ago. 'Evangelisation', as a Church activity, has taken on a complexity that matches that of the complexity of professional leadership in education. Also, the new generation of lay principals are not immune to the changes in religious sensibility in Irish culture. They too have been affected by changing attitudes towards power, institutions, moral values and personal fulfilment. Many have not been encouraged to express their own spirituality in a public forum, much less lead others in finding expression for a deeper spiritual experience. There is an emerging need to integrate a personal and professional spirituality into the training of leaders for Catholic schools.

The changes that have taken place since the 1970s in the profile of members of religious congregations committed to working in schools is not simply a matter of numbers. It also encompasses new approaches to spirituality within these congregations. With government involvement and commitment to mass education, the focus of Christian witness to more marginalised members of society changed. Although education remains a key factor in promotion and mobility in society, equality of opportunity is now being provided as part of public policy. Equity in the consumption of such opportunities still remains problematic, and many religious congregations have adopted a more pastoral (as opposed to institutional) approach to helping people avail of the educational resources made available by the state. They see their role now more as influencing values through community development and encouragement, rather than through administrative control of schools.

The soul-searching engaged in by most religious congregations and the search for a more authentic witness to gospel values has led to a new theology and renewal of religious life. Unfortunately, some of the apostolic works undertaken by the religious congregations were not renewed in the same way. Rather, the validity of involvement in many traditional works has been questioned. This has been particularly true of education and health care, which have a major institutional dimension to them. One argument is that running such institutions draws the congregation into issues of power and control, rather than direct service. Another critique is that Church involvement in these institutions has contributed to maintaining a social profile based on sectarian or class divisions. In particular, the origin of the education system in Ireland has been based in the sectarian politics of the nineteenth century and there is a strong confessional element in the history of Catholic self-identity in the schools. Congregational involvement in education was definitely part of an 'Education for Catholics' movement. The aim was to promote a social mobility for Catholics, so that they could play a part in the political arena, ensuring the role of the Church in that arena. In religious education at secondary level, there seems to have been a greater emphasis on apologetics than on scripture. This would help the student be more articulate in debating social and moral issues from the Catholic perspective.

Following from this context, the focus of reflection has been external, promoting the right of the Church to be involved in schooling in a pluralist society. This contrasts with a more internal focus that looks at the nature of 'Catholic Education for All". This approach seeks to develop a new theology and spirituality *of* education and schooling, rather than look at theology and spirituality *in* education. Church documents such as *Declaration on Christian Education* (1965), *The Catholic School* (1977), *Lay Catholics in Schools: Witness to Faith* (1982), *The Religious Dimension of Education in a Catholic School* (1988), *The Catholic School on the Threshold of the Third Millennium* (1998) affirmed the work of education, and particularly the role of the lay teachers in that work. The presentation remains on the general level of a positive philosophy of the human person, with a consequent demand for holistic education and an emphasis on good human relationships within the school as a witness to gospel values. Where reference is paid to modern culture, the focus is on secularising influences and their impact on the work of evangelisation in schools. Little attention has been paid to the impact of new technologies and economies on the role of education in personal and national development, and little effort has been made to address the integration of these developments into a Catholic vision of education. One frequently has the impression that the humanism of the Enlightenment and the Renaissance is still the paradigm from which Catholic philosophy of education is developed.

Another criticism of Church involvement in schools is that it is an exercise in institutional self-deception. Pride in the attractiveness of Catholic education to a large number of parents is criticised as a denial of the alienation of many Church members. The quality of many Catholic schools draws students from a wide section of the community, and the claim is that sheer weight of numbers gives an illusion of vibrancy. There is a growing awareness among Catholic educators that numbers are not enough. There is a need to focus on the ethos and values that are being communicated through the schooling process. This impetus has come mainly from countries in which the Catholic Church is a minority, and where there is clear separation of Catholic and public education. In particular there is a growing body of literature on Catholic education, and leadership in Catholic schools, from the United States, Canada, Australia and the United Kingdom.

A central theme in this literature is the development of leadership spirituality. This is not simply an academic approach to understanding Catholic values in a secular education system. Rather it is a personal response to and support of those people who exercise school leadership as part of their personal commitment to God and their ministry within the Church. This book arises out of that tradition. For a number of years, I have been working with the education offices of religious congregations. In working with the Presentation Sisters, Northern Province, we have focused on the role of the Catholic school in faith development. With principals and deputy principals, and more recently with members of boards of management, we have explored various dimensions of personal growth and faith development, and how this is integrated into leadership roles in schools. One of the most fruitful parts of our time together has been learning to pray over scripture texts related to leadership and vision, and sharing insights with one another. This has been both personal (related to the person of the leader) and practical (reflecting on policies for faith formation in the schools). One of the aims of this book is to share these exercises with a wider audience and to promote a level of personal and shared reflection on how the mission of teaching and leadership in schools can be articulated in Ireland at the beginning of the twenty-first century. Hopefully, those who engage with the exercises in the book, either as individuals or as a group, will find personal benefit and support. A second aim is, as mentioned above, to help develop a *theology of* education (an integrated, personal dimension) as well as a *theology in* education (a practical, product dimension), which will guide responses to the pastoral needs of those engaged in Catholic education in the future.

The next chapter explores some of the insights we have developed already on the role of spirituality in personal and professional development. In particular, the chapter explores different approaches to a personal spirituality, to work in general and particularly to teaching and leadership.

The rest of the book is divided into six sections, each of which allows the reader to explore different perspectives of educational leadership.

- Call
- Vision
- Leadership Style
- Discipline and Pastoral Care
- Teaching as Leadership
- Jesus as Role Model

Each section begins with a short exposition of the theme of the section, based on scripture. Then there are a number of scripture passages, each with a set of questions to promote reflection. The choice of scripture and the questions are not prescriptive. They simply set the tone for personal reflection.

Please feel free to use other passages or other questions. In particular, some of the scripture outlined in the introduction to the section could well serve as material for your reflections. The exercises are not exams, and you do not have to cover all the questions at any one time. If a question inspires you to reflect on your own life, your own work or a particular event, stay with it. Depth is more fruitful than breadth in dealing with the Holy Spirit!

How to use this book

This book can be used in a variety of ways. You may want to approach this book as an individual. Another approach is to find a group of colleagues who are interested in exploring the themes together. A third approach might be as a training exercise, for example with a board of management, a management team in the school or maybe a group of parent or student leaders (e.g. Parents' Association or Student Council). They agree to set aside some of their time together to reflect on issues related to Catholic education, and apply it to their work.

Individuals

Some readers may want to explore the texts as part of their personal journey. For them, one way of using the book is to set some time aside on a regular basis to pray, reflect or journal about the themes. If you want to take this approach, then decide on a regular time – every day, every week or even once a month. Decide in advance on what exercise you want to do – do not skip between them. Make sure you can be quiet and uninterrupted for that time.

Take a moment to relax, and focus on why you are doing this exercise. Then slowly read the passage of scripture and reflect on what it means for you. If you need some help, then read through the questions. If one of them strikes a chord, then stay with that question and tease it out in the context of the scripture passage. See if the passage consoles you, affirms you or maybe challenges you. A good way of doing this is to journal – to write your responses.

When the time you set aside is nearly over, then pause again and reflect what this exercise has meant for you. If you feel like praying, then this might be a good time to turn to God and speak about what you have felt and experienced.

With some practice, you may not need a scripture passage or questions to help you. Your own experience will be material enough for reflection. You might read over your journal for the past week or month, and discover patterns there that are worth exploring in depth. There may also be questions that you have avoided dealing with – they can be points for fruitful reflection as well. If you want further support, then you may seek out new reading material, or new sources of help.

Support groups
A fruitful way of exploring the themes in this book is with the help of others in a group. A group of friends and colleagues agree to meet on a regular basis and explore the themes together and share the personal meaning they have as teachers or leaders. These might be teachers in the same school, or a group of teachers from different schools who share a common friendship or professional interest (same subject, principals).

There are two ways in which a group like this might work. The first would be that the group both reflects and shares together. One person takes responsibility for organising a meeting place and for choosing the theme for the session. They may want to adapt some of the questions in the book to make them more relevant to the local situation.

It is important that the location offers some privacy, quiet and freedom from distraction. A quiet room, with a candle lighting on a table, is often used. After a brief introduction and quiet period where the individuals in the group relax and focus, the scripture passage is read. This is followed by a period of silence in which individuals reflect on the scripture and perhaps on some of the questions. Each person then has the opportunity to share their reflections – what struck them about the passage. When everyone has had a chance to share, there might be some general discussion on themes that arose during the sharing. The session might end with a short prayer from the leader.

A second approach to group work is to ask individuals to reflect on set passages of scripture before the meeting. For instance, a group might choose the theme of vision for their monthly meeting. Each member would explore the same scripture passages between meetings. When the group comes together, the meeting might start with a period of quiet prayer or reflection. During the meeting, each member would share reflections on what they had noticed over the previous month, perhaps followed by some discussion. The meeting might end with a prayer.

Teams

The approach to working with teams is similar to working as a support group. However, the focus of the sharing might be more applied and practical than personal. A board of management might set aside fifteen minutes or half an hour on a regular basis to reflect on ethos issues within the school. Members might be asked to spend some time reflecting on one scripture passage, or maybe a number of passages, before they come to the meeting. Each person is then invited to share on the practical consequences of their reflections. For instance, they might reflect on their own need for further information about scripture, or a Catholic philosophy of education, or the ethos of the school. They might propose looking at some school policies in the light of values that emerged in their reflections.

Each of the sharing sessions might be proceeded and ended by a quiet period of prayer. Also, members need not be constrained by the practical. They are also free to share on the personal meaning of the scripture – for instance, as it applies to their sense of mission. However, the main aim of this type of group is to develop the ethos of the school in a reflective way, where time and priority is given to finding direction for the future through gospel values.

SPIRITUALITY AND LEADERS

When we think of leadership in schools, we generally focus on the principal. It is sometimes claimed that the principal is 'the single most important factor' in excellent schools. This places the burden and the mystique of leadership on a single individual. The principal is seen as vision setter, instructional leader, staff developer, chief executive and occasionally 'all of the above'. However, in schools, there is wide scope for leadership outside the formal position of the principal – what Raelin called 'Leaderful Organisations'[1]. Individual teachers may exercise an informal leadership function with their peers because of their expertise or status. Others exercise a leadership role for students in their teaching or in extra-curricular activities. Students may exercise a formal leadership role as prefects or members of a student council. They also work at an informal level, especially in the way senior students may be role models for juniors. When leadership is considered from the perspective of vision and inspiration, rather than as a 'job' within the school, all members of a school community have an opportunity to reflect on their own leadership function and style, and their contribution to the overall vision of the school. They renew or re-evaluate how they choose to exercise that leadership function. Leadership becomes a shared activity, applying to board members, principals, teachers, parents and students where the guiding light is the agreed common vision to which the school aspires. When this vision is guided by Gospel values, then shared reflection on the gospel narrative can serve to clarify, validate and occasionally challenge personal and school visions.

Christian spirituality draws its inspiration from the story of God at work with his people, especially in the life of Jesus. The mission and ministry of Jesus is celebrated and lived out by the Christian community, inspired by the Holy Spirit who has been promised as a gift 'to be with us until the end of time'. Ministers in that community, because of their positions and the demands of their roles, require a particularly shaped spirituality. Their spirituality is built around their own human development, their view of work and how it contributes to their spirituality, and particularly the joys and pains of their roles as leaders. In this chapter, we outline some aspects of that spiritual journey.

Personal spirituality

Spirituality has been defined in many different ways. From one perspective, it is the lived dimension of faith. It is how faith looks in everyday relationships, attitudes, values and behaviours. It is the set of assumptions an individual lives out of, and where he or she chooses to locate meaning. For the Christian, this works on both a communal and personal level. The meaning of life is centred on a God who sent the Son and the Spirit to save his people and be with them. A personal spirituality emerges in the dialogue between this communal faith story and the concrete events of each individual's life experience.

Since Vatican II, there has been a radical shift in the understanding of spirituality. The clear distinctions that were made between body and spirit, between the sacred and the secular, no longer hold. There was a time when the Church was seen as a place of grace, and the world as a place of sin. Christians came to the Church for a refill of grace to sustain them in a hostile, secular world. The shift with Vatican II was to affirm the world as grace-filled. It was created by God, redeemed by Jesus and the Holy Spirit lives in it. This makes the world the first arena for experiencing God's grace, for grace builds on nature. 'Church' emerges out of that experience. In church, Christians name, symbolise and celebrate the God they have found in their daily lives.

Spirituality is an essential dimension of being human. It encompasses an understanding of God, self, other people and the world. In includes the way actions and relationships develop because of these understandings and involves a search for authenticity between this understanding, and the way life is lived. O'Murchú claims

> The spiritual thirst of humanity is for an integrated and coherent comprehension of life; it expresses a profound human need to hold together in some type of creative synthesis the polarities and contradictions of human experience.[2]

Spirituality therefore is not an added extra to life, a kind of decoration that brightens it up. Rather, it is the leaven of life itself. It gives depth, meaning and resonance to the ordinary in life. We find spiritual inspiration in our experiences of friendship and reconciliation. Our own experiences of loving and nurturing a partner or a child, and our sense of being unconditionally loved by another, are deep human experiences that develop our sensibilities to the loving action of God in our lives. Similarly, our ability to read literature and poetry and listen to music develops our capacity to enter into new worlds and be caught up in the mystery of human existence. This experience is a vital factor in our ability to sense the transcendence of God and our own invitation to transcendence. Our understanding of science and history brings us in touch with the mystery of the universe and the struggle to be human in that universe. This also leads us to a sense of wonder at the purpose of life, in all its complexity and mystery. Our personal spirituality involves how we are present to, and make sense of, the profound realities of our lives. We give expression to our deepest meanings through commonly held, but often poorly articulated, symbols. These frequently revolve around rituals relating to birth and death, and in rites of passage of adult life. In dealing with personal spirituality here, I want to focus on one small perspective – that of hope and optimism in what we do.

Gallagher,[3] commenting on the crisis in faith in the post-modern world, notes two trends emerging from the rejection of previous certainties about the positive interpretation of human development in the use of reason and science and at claims to social progress through history. One trend is to describe humankind as having fallen into deeper isolation, fragmentation and narcissism. At one level, this gives rise to nihilism and doubts about truth and value. At another level, life is seen as an indifferent game and individual values are merely aesthetic and provisional. The consequence is that values are superficial and the individual is passive and apathetic, with a floating lifestyle and provisional commitment. A second trend is more constructive, and indicates that the sense of self gives rise to hope for the future. A search for meaning arises out of the permanent hungers of the heart. This finds expression in a personal stance and lifestyle embedded in a new honesty and humility as the individual seeks liberation and authenticity.

This tension between a negative and positive perspective on the human condition is nothing new. It has a long history, and can be found in the early chapters of the Book of Genesis. There we have two different accounts of the creation story. The first sees humankind in partnership with a creative God, who is constantly at work, leading his people to salvation. The second is more pessimistic, and is based on the story of the fall of Adam and Eve from divine favour and how the consequences of their sin was visited on future generations, so that not only humankind, but all creation, is seen as flawed.

Each of these spiritualities has a particular emphasis and language. The writings of Fox, de Mello and O'Donoghue are in the first tradition, where they seek to develop an inner-centred spirituality, where meaning is found in every routine, and there is a basic optimism about human experience. Most people over thirty have been exposed to the second spirituality. This has a focus on humanity's weakness and need for redemption. The main symbol of this spirituality is the Cross, where suffering is seen as the punishment and expiation for sin. In response we are encouraged to seek redemption through abnegation of the flesh in penance and private devotions. The soul is seen as trapped by the weak body, whose corrupting influence should be lessened.

Both these spiritualities have different balances in the emphasis on transcendence and immanence, which gives rise to qualitatively different relationships with God. In our spirituality we must deal with three time frames. The **past** is interpreted to show how God revealed himself through history (Heb 1:1). It promotes a sense of community identity, and names heroes and role models within the community. A focus on the **present** seeks to provide experiences and rituals that connect the individual with the central vision of the community, and to help members live according to these insights. The focus on the

future looks to the promise that accompanies faithful and authentic discipleship.

Yesterday	that which must be connected with – the fundamentalism of Christian narrative.
Today	that which must be attended to, and the belief that the Spirit is still present and developing the Christian tradition.
Tomorrow	towards which we are oriented in the promise of the Kingdom and heaven.[4]

A key challenge for individual spirituality is to understand the forces that trap us in one orientation rather than another. For instance, we can take comfort in the certainties of the past. Our history can be revisionist, remembering only the good parts. We spend our time reminiscing about the past. Others may despair of the present, especially the changing values of society, and particularly of young people. They focus their hope on some distant time in the future, when all will be well. Thus, they avoid the pain of the present moment.

For others, the challenge of personal growth is fragmented. They grow in different ways in different areas of their lives. For instance, a teacher may grow in technical competence, able to explain material and help students achieve at a high level. Yet, the same teacher may fail to develop meaningful ways of relating to students as the age difference between themselves and the students widens. Other teachers may become disenchanted with the world of school, getting bogged down in the repetitious nature of teaching. They find life and growth outside the school, with their family or in other aspects of their social lives. In these cases, what happens is that people call a moratorium on growth in particular areas of their lives. In effect, this means that their lives are fragmented. They become different people depending on who they are with or where they are.

A challenge for all of us is to integrate different areas of our lives – our work, our family, our leisure. We need to grow in our relationships with other people and with God. Growth in one area can challenge our ways of working in other areas. For instance, when we are young, we are dependent on our parents for many things. We ask permission to go out; we ask for money to buy things and go places. However, as we grow older, we become more independent. The relationship changes. We no longer ask for things. Our conversation can be more adult. Similarly, our relationship with God also changes. As young people, we can see God as a parent who sets rules and who grants favours when we pray. As we grow older, we come to realise that 'bad things happen to good people', and that God does not always answer our prayers as we would wish. We need to develop new images of God and a new way of relating to him. In the next two sections of this chapter, we explore different challenges in developing our approach to work and to leadership.

Spirituality of work

A key element in developing a spirituality related to the work we do as teachers or leaders is to understand the place of work in a spiritual framework. In this section, a short outline is given of different historical approaches to a theology of work. Hopefully, this forms the basis for further reflection on the role of leadership in education.

In the account of creation in the early chapters of the Book of Genesis, we find two perspectives on work. In the first of these, we are told that 'Yahweh God took the man and settled him in the garden of Eden to cultivate and take care of it' (2:15). This account is part of a very positive perspective on the role of humankind in creation. God made humankind (male and female) in his own image (1:27), and, having set the universe in place, entrusted it to them 'to fill the earth and conquer it, to be masters of the fish of the sea and the birds of the air and all living animals on the earth' (1:28).

The second perspective looks on work as a punishment resulting from the Fall. As a result of their sin, God proclaimed that man and woman would be enemies of one another. The woman would suffer as mother and wife through the pains of childbirth, and the man was punished as a bread-winner through the pain and frustration of work.

> Accursed be the soil because of you. With suffering shall you get your food from it every day of your life. It shall yield you brambles and thistles, and you shall eat wild plants. With sweat on your brow shall you eat your bread until you return to the soil as you were taken from it'. (3:17-19)

To these specific penalties were added death and loss of intimacy with God.

Throughout the Old Testament, we have various testimonies to both these traditions about work. The curse of work is seen in the slavery endured in Egypt and later in Babylon. Injustice and greed frequently made work a crushing burden and a source of hatred and division. Greedy employers deprived workers of their pay (Jer 22:13) for their own gain, and rulers levied unjust taxes against the poor to support their own luxury (Amos 5:11). Although success was frequently experienced, and good work accomplished, the wise man reflected on the futility of it all.

> Hence I have come to despair of all the efforts I have expended under the sun. For so it is that a man who has laboured wisely, skilfully and successfully must leave what is his own to

someone who has not toiled for it at all. This, too, is vanity and great injustice; for what does he gain for all the toil and strain that he has undergone under the sun? What of all his laborious days, his cares of office, his restless nights? This too is vanity. There is no happiness for man but to eat and drink and to be content with his work. This, too, I see as something from God's hand, since plenty and penury both come from God; Wisdom, knowledge, joy, he gives to the man who pleases him. On the sinner lays the task of gathering and storing up for another who is pleasing to God. (Eccl 2:20-25)

The positive perspective on work is often seen in the imagery attached to its description. The ten commandments proclaim a Sabbath, which reflects the creative activity of God, who worked for six days and then rested. God is portrayed as a busy worker on behalf of his people (Ps. 104, 105), which distinguishes him from the other gods. God gives people the 'skill and perception and knowledge for every kind of craft' (Ex. 31:2) so that they use their gift for his purpose. In Jeremiah 18:1-12, the work of the potter is a parable of God making the nations. The prophet consistently performs or interprets symbolic actions related to the ordinary work of the people – the yoke as a symbol of slavery (27-28) and buying a field as an act of confidence in the future (32). In the psalms, 'Yahweh is my Shepherd' depicts God's care as human work. In the community, work has an aesthetic and social value. Work well done gives glory to God, and through it, an individual plays a productive role. The person who is idle is not living up to his potential, and is liable to starve, and occasionally we find people who misuse their creative powers in fashioning idols.

In John's gospel, we find Jesus very strongly focused on doing the work of the Father. He is frequently portrayed as doing this work on a Sabbath, thus claiming the privilege of the Creator. His miracles signify a power over creation and his mission is a sign that God is no longer resting, but working again to reclaim creation. In the New Testament, Jesus uses the world of work as a metaphor for his own mission. He describes himself as a shepherd, a vine-dresser, a doctor, a sower. His work, and that of the disciples, is harvesting. They also become fishers of men. When he speaks of the life of the Spirit, he links the audience to their experience of work – as farmers, housewives, builders, bakers, servants, and as soldiers. However, he also warns people 'Do not work for food that cannot last, but work for food that endures to eternal life' (Jn 6:27). It is not that food, drink and clothing are unimportant, but a preoccupation with them may mean that one can gain the whole world, but lose the kingdom of God (Lk 9:25).

The early Church inherited ambivalent values towards work. The monastic tradition affirmed the dignity of work. The Benedictine motto is 'To Work is to Pray'. Aquinas taught that every single person is called to work according to his or her role in society and the fulfilment of these roles leads to justice in society. In Medieval times, workers were organised in guilds to encourage a religious sense of work.

However, another tradition was more pessimistic. The Greeks saw work as the domain of slaves. This was reinforced in dualistic ideals which saw the soul or spirit as the essence of being and the body and material things as corrupt. Work was associated with the flesh and seen as the consequence of sin. However, by working in such a way as to submit the flesh to the punishment due for sin, the soul was purified for heaven.

This redemptive theology dominated Church thinking from the time of Augustine. This led to a focus on personal salvation rather than community well being. The individual engaged in 'good works' as a sign of repentance and expiation of the effects of sin, rather than seeing their work as a partnership with God in the building up of the Christian community. When this world view came under pressure through the scientific and industrial revolution, the Church reacted very defensively and found it difficult to integrate the new challenges into its philosophical viewpoint. It is only in the face of emerging ideologies of capitalism and communism, the growing gap between rich and poor and the impact of industrial development on the environment, that the Church has begun to develop a more comprehensive and creation-centred approach to work. This celebrates the world as the richness of God's creation, and work shares in the ongoing evolution of the creative energies in the universe. This view of the world and of work stands as counter to an economic view of the world, which sees work as a mere instrument of production, in which consumerism is the ultimate human value.

When leaders therefore reflect on work, they reflect on themselves as workers, and how their own work achieves something very practical, and at the same time releases in them a power and capacity for creativity. This creativity expresses itself in their own growth and learning, and in promoting the growth and learning of others.

In schools, there is a need to develop some reflection on what is meant by work. One of the main expectations of schools is that they prepare their students for the world of work. Having a shared vision of what work and career is shapes student attitudes to career, competition, co-operation, and service. It influences choices of subjects and the criteria used in evaluating career choices. If a Christian theology of work, based on shared partnership with God in the creative evolution of the universe, is promoted and accepted, then new partnerships and relationships between principals and teachers, between teachers and students, and between school and family are possible. A spirituality of work not only affects the individual teacher, student or parent leader, the principal or board member. It also affects the vision and paradigm of education itself.

Spirituality of leadership

Leadership studies have generally focused on the leader-follower relationship, where the leader was seen to motivate followers to bring about intended outcomes and to reward them appropriately. The leader was seen to own a vision or a plan, and through the right balance of authority and participation, empowered the followers to achieve something they could not do on their own.

Bennis distinguished administrators as those who 'do the thing right' and leaders as those who 'do the right thing'. The focus here is on the distinction between efficiency and effectiveness in organisational planning and development. Bolman and Deal have typified the work of the leadership as a balance between logic and artistry, drawing attention to the importance of the symbolic in bringing meaning and energy to the day-to-day technical processes of the school. Duignan and McPherson have developed a model of educative leadership that focuses on three areas – things, people and ideas – with the aim of cultivating a sense of purpose in the school. Sergiovanni focused on the moral dimension of leadership and the responsibility of the leader to articulate and promote an inclusive vision that represents the community. Sergiovanni used the religious term 'covenant' to depict the relationship between leader and community [5]

Earlier, Sergiovanni[6] had outlined five forces or skills that leaders use in schools. The first two of these he termed technical and human. These refer to the transactional skills related to task – planning, organising, coordinating – and human relations – encouraging, building morale, using participation, managing conflict and, in general, enabling people to attain satisfaction. The other three skills were conceptual skills. The first of these he termed education, which derives from expert knowledge about learning and schooling. Principals are regarded as instructional leaders within the school and they exercise their expertise in terms of programme development and teacher supervision. This expert knowledge helps a principal judge the importance and relevance of different practices and to promote particular approaches to school development. This type of expert skill can be applied to other leaders in the school, as they link activities to the main purpose of the school.

A second conceptual skill is symbolic. Principals focus attention on matters of importance to the school, and they also model behaviours and values. Thus, where the principal spends time and energy is a powerful symbol of what is important. Symbolic leaders constantly seek rituals and ceremonies that are congruent with the important values and the vision of the school. The third conceptual skill is what Sergiovanni termed cultural. This involves building a unique school culture and includes creating, nurturing and teaching the organisational story of the school. It involves the articulation of the school mission, the induction and socialisation of new members to the story, as well as reinforcing the beliefs and traditions within the school. This function builds the unique identity of the school.

For Sergiovanni, all five skills – the technical, human, education, symbolic and cultural – are essential elements of leadership and they build on one another. The traditional emphasis on the technical, human and education is essential, he claimed, for competent schools. However, there are schools that wish to go beyond competence and pursue excellence. They develop a love of learning greater than academic performance and achievement. In these schools, great attention is paid to symbolic and cultural development. Symbolic and cultural forces build on the other three, and in turn, nurture them.

Starratt used the metaphor of drama to illustrate the person of the leader. Drama deals with ordinary events and emotions in the lives of the audience and puts them together in an intense experience.[7] This forces the audience to experience these events in a different way and to look at them with different eyes and perhaps to see a new way of responding to them. In a sense, the drama both specifies and reframes the context of the experiences, giving the audience a new perspective and a new perception of what is happening in critical events. The leader also exercises a similar role. He or she interprets the events of the school in such a way as to clarify their meaning or the drama of the challenge they offer. This helps those in the school to enter into their experience of education in a deeper and more empowered manner. However, leadership is more than just a prophetic role that interprets the events of the day. It requires the ability to find ways that structure this vision, that give it some form of permanence and at the same time allows it to be reviewed and restated periodically. The drama of leadership requires a writer, a producer, a director, actors, and an audience, and people in the school can play each of these roles at different times.

Each leader is involved in three sets of drama –

- their own personal development;
- seeing development in their colleagues;
- facilitating the development of colleagues.

Reflection on these different roles has sometimes been imaged as leaders acting as different archetypes. Understanding leadership in terms of archetypes has been a trend in research for some time. Thomas Carlyle defined the archetype as a 'symbol system' that guided the leader's performance. He was convinced that:

> It is in and through symbols that man, consciously or unconsciously, lives, works and has his meaning.[8]

He defined the leader in terms of the hero, and uses the archetypes of divinity, poet, priest, prophet, man of letters and king to capture different types of hero. This approach to leadership builds on a long tradition of developing myths and legends that portray different archetypes of hero on a grand adventure. In the *Odyssey*, Odysseus fought to overcome obstacles in order to reinstate stability, order and purpose in Ithaca, and a major part of his struggle was the journey home. In the *Divine Comedy*, the hero searched for a pathway leading from chaos to unity. Parzival, as a knight of the Round Table, sought to overcome his own limitations in the search for the Holy Grail. In Tolkien's *Lord of the Rings* Bilbo Baggins and his nephew Frodo must leave the Shire and Bag End for their adventure, even though Bilbo's first reaction when Gandalf the wizard suggested an adventure, was to reject the idea:

> 'We are plain quiet folk and have no use for adventures, nasty disturbing uncomfortable things! Make you late for dinner! I can't see what anybody sees in them.'[9]

Luke Skywalker in *Star Wars* fought 'the dark side' and his own despair at its power. Harry Potter had to accept his own history of being a wizard and faced his battle with Voldemort aided by Hermione and Ron, under the watchful eye of Professor Dumbledore. The hero is not someone born with charismatic leadership qualities. He is an ordinary character, and the adventure brings forth a personal transformation that allows heroic characteristics to develop. The mythic journey is therefore a parable of all our lives, a universal journey toward self-realisation, as we struggle with who we are and why we are here.[10]

The adventure starts in the home ground, and consists of setting out to search for, and bring back, an object of great value to benefit the home community. The Holy Grail was the quest of the Arthurian knights, while the quest of the Fellowship in Tolkien's *Lord of the Rings* was to destroy the Ring. This is a tangible object that resonates with multiple layers of meaning that have personal (for the hero) and communal significance. The hero often displays some reluctance to leave the home ground before being convinced to do so. This reluctance often leads to a fellowship of travellers, as he is accompanied by others from the community. When he leaves, the hero frequently has to confront a guardian of the outer world. This guardian takes the form of a dragon, a demon or some other monster. This guardian is not to be killed, but must be confronted. Along his journey, the hero has to face multiple internal and external tests of faith and discipline. His quest is both in service of the home ground, and also mastery of his own inner life. In order to do this, the hero needs help, and frequently makes an alliance with a guide who knows the ways of the outer world, and who has the gift of wisdom. Meanwhile, the home ground is guarded by warriors. Their function is to ensure that the home ground still exists on the hero's successful return.

Recent literature on leadership has revisited the idea of a mythic journey. Dunlop[11] draws parallels between the hero's journey and the task of delivering results of major innovation in the world of business. Brown and Moffett[12] draw parallels between the elements of heroic journeys and present day school reform. Parallels can be found in Bolman and Deal, in Deal and Peterson and in Palmer.[13]

To some extent, elements of these mythical stories have given rise to the different themes explored in the next sections. The first of these is that of the call to leadership, and how we experience the invitation to take on this journey. The second theme is that of vision, and seeks to define the treasure for which we seek. A third theme looks at styles of leadership, and looks at how a leader makes the journey – the friends that are brought along and the guides that are used. Themes 4 and 5 look at particular aspects of the school – the role of discipline, pastoral care and teaching. This looks at how the leader might face the different dragons and guardians of the outer world – whether he seeks to confront or to kill them. The final theme turns to look at Jesus as the model for our own leadership.

Notes

1   Raelin, J., *Creating Leaderful Organizations: How to bring out leadership in everyone.* San Francisco: Berret-Koehler Publishers, 2003.

2   O'Murchú, *The God Who Becomes Redundant*, Dublin: Mercier Press. p. 42, 1986.

3   Gallagher, M.P. (1996) 'Post Modernity: Friend or Foe?' in Cassidy, E. (1996) *Faith and Culture in the Irish Context.* Dublin: Veritas. pp 71-82

4   Based on Holly, M. and Walley, C., 'Teachers as Professionals' in Holly, M. and McLoughlin, C. (Eds.) *Perspectives on Teacher Professional Development.* London: Falmer. p. 285, 1989.

5   Bennis, W., *On Becoming a Leader,* Reading, MA: Addison-Wesley 1989; Bolman, L.G. and Deal. T.E., *Reframing Organizations: Artistry, Choice and Leadership,* San Francisco: Jossey-Bass, 1991; Duignan, P. and MacPherson, R.J.S., *Educative Leadership,* London: Falmer Press, 1992; Sergiovanni, T.H., *Moral Leadership,* San Francisco: Jossey-Bass, 1992.

6   Sergiovanni, T.J., 'Leadership and Excellence in schooling', *Educational Leadership,* 1984, 41:4-43.

7   Starratt, R.J., *The Drama of Leadership,* London: Falmer Press, 1993.

8   Carlyle, T., *Heroes and Hero-worship,* London: Routledge Universal Library Series, 1841

9   Tolkien, J.R.R., *The Hobbitt,* Boston: Houghton Mifflin Co., 1937.

10 Campbell, J. and Moyers, B., *The Power of Myth.* New York: Doubleday, 1988. Feinstein, D. and Krippner, S. *The Mythic Path.* New York, Tarcher/Putnam: 1997. Katzenmeyer, M. and Moller, G., *Awakening the Sleeping Giant; Leadership Development for Teachers.* Thousand Oaks, CA: Corwin Press, 1996. Pearson, C.S., *Awakening the Heroes within: twelve archetypes to help us find ourselves and transform our world,* San Francisco: Harper Collins, 1991.

11 Dunlop, S. *Business Heroes,* Oxford: Copstone, 1997.

12 Brown, J.L. and Moffett, C.A. *The Hero's Journey. How educators can transform schools and improve learning.* Alexandria, VA: ASCD, 1999. Deal, T.E. and Peterson, K.D., *The Leadership Paradox,* San Francisco: Jossey-Bass, 1994.

13 Bolman, L.G., and Deal, T.E. *Leading with Soul; An uncommon journey of spirit.* San Francisco: Jossey-Bass, 1995. Palmer, *Courage to Teacher: Exploring the Inner Landscape of a Teacher's Life,* San Francisco: Jossey-Bass, 1997.

THE CALL TO LEADERSHIP

> Do not be afraid of greatness. Some are born
> great, some achieve greatness and some have
> greatness thrust upon them.[1]

The scriptures tell us of many different leaders in the history of
Israel and in the early Church. Some of these people seem to
have been born with great leadership qualities (Saul, Joshua,
Samson in the Old Testament, and Paul in the New). There are
also plenty of examples of those who were not obvious leaders,
and who seemed to 'emerge out of nowhere' to take on an
important leadership role and meet a need in the faith
community of the time (Moses, David, Jeremiah in the Old
Testament and the apostles in the New Testament). For all of
these people, their leadership was seen as a gift from God. This
gift was made known to them in a call to serve a particular
function or perform a specific task on God's behalf, and was
confirmed by a heightened sense of God's presence with them
as they performed their role.

As the history of Israel unfolded, different forms of
leadership emerged. In the early days, the focus was on great
men. These were the Patriarchs of the Chosen People who
responded in faith to God's initiative and self-revelation.
Abraham, Isaac and Jacob built up a community of believers

who were faithful to the One God, who made a covenant with them that he would be active on their behalf. The faith of the community was soon tested. Early prosperity gave way to captivity and slavery in Egypt. Then God took pity on his people and led them to freedom, promising them entry to the Promised Land. This promise required a new kind of leadership, and we see this first in charismatic figures such as Moses and Joshua, and later in the great kings, Saul, David and Solomon who established Israel as a nation. These were leaders chosen to perform great deeds. They had powerful signs that God was with them, clearing their enemies before them. Their leadership was experienced as a special call, although this was not always a personal call. For instance, David's call was mediated through Samuel, although his work as king was accompanied by a special relationship with God.

As the kingdom of Israel became established, two leadership functions emerged in the community – the king and the priest. The king became the adopted son of God. God promised that he would protect the king if he was faithful, and assured prosperity and justice for the people by victory over external and internal enemies. This linked the role of the king with the covenant. The priesthood was established in rather gory circumstances in the time of Moses (Ex 32:25-29) and the tribe of Levi was specially consecrated to exercise its functions. The priest presided over the worship of the community and acted as a mediator between the people and God through the ritual of sacrifice, reciting the narrative of the covenant (Torah) and communicated the divine blessing to the people.

Both these functions were hereditary. The kingdom of Israel split in two, and bad kings emerged in both kingdoms. They copied the kings of their neighbours, especially in an idolatry that regarded royalty as divine, instead of receiving its mission from God. Similarly, we read of priests who failed to nourish the people because of their own lack of commitment (Hos 4:4-11). In the midst of this, a third form of leadership emerged – that of prophet. Prophets were specially called by God and prompted by his spirit. They were to pass on the Word to the whole community. 'Hear, O Israel' was a common theme among all the Old Testament prophets. They reminded the people of their covenant pledge. They also interpreted the meaning of that call within the historical circumstances of each age.

In the New Testament, Jesus exercises his leadership as Priest, Prophet and King. In his death, he is the priest of his own sacrifice, bringing about the salvation of his people. In this function, he also comes to fulfil the Law (the Torah) by showing its richness, and by transcending it in the law of love. Jesus also acted as a prophet. His actions against authority and hypocrisy were very much in the prophetic tradition. He had received his message from the Father, and he spoke with authority in making known the signs of the times, and proclaiming the fulfilment of God's promises. His preaching was accompanied by signs and miracles, and the people proclaimed him as a prophet (Jn 4:19). Jesus exercised his kingship in a way that is totally different from a secular understanding. He had been sent by the Father, and he was the true Son of God. His mission was to preach the kingdom, but he specified that his kingdom was not of this world, and not in competition with that of Caesar. At his death, he was ironically proclaimed as 'King of the Jews' and spoke of how he would enter into his true glory after his death, where he would later come again in judgement.

From the very beginning of his public life, Jesus wanted to have others with him and to multiply his presence. He seemed to have two levels of special followers – disciples and apostles. When he sent them on a mission, they were to speak in his name, with his authority (Mt. 10:40). The selection of the twelve had a special symbolic significance in constituting the new Israel, and they were to witness that the risen Christ was the same Jesus they had lived with. Hence their calling involved a long apprenticeship in understanding the message of Jesus, and learning who he was.

The New Testament also bears witness to a more gentle form of leadership. If the role of leadership is seen as a call to understand the values of Jesus, develop a relationship with him and witness to his presence in the world, we find that among a number of women in the scriptures. In the resurrection stories, Jesus shows himself first to Mary of Magdala, Joanna and Mary the mother of James, who then raced to tell the apostles (Lk 24:1-11). Mary of Magdala had heard her call in the forgiveness she experienced from Jesus. But the greatest witness to Jesus was his mother Mary. It was her 'yes' that allowed Jesus come into the world. She nurtured him through childhood and taught him to be human. She pondered all the events of his life in her heart, and faithfully followed him to the cross. She acts as the signpost and model for the Church in its work of revealing Jesus to others.

In Vatican II, the document *Lumen Gentium* (34-36) reflects on the way the laity is called to share in the three roles of Priest, Prophet and King through their baptism, and how our personalities, our daily lives and above all our daily work witnesses to and promotes each of these elements of the Christian mission to sanctify, to teach and to rule. In considering the spirituality of leaders earlier, we saw how archetypes are a key to understanding the role of leadership. These three roles are the archetypes of scripture, and we return to them in more detail in Theme 3, on leadership styles.

In this section, you are asked to reflect on the sense of call to leadership. In the events we have outlined above, most of the

LEADING LIFE TO THE FULL

individuals had a strong sense of individual call and election by God. This was central to their leadership. From the Old Testament, we have chosen one leader, Moses, from among those who were called to perform great deeds, and one, Jeremiah, from the prophetic tradition. In the New Testament, we have chosen the call of the first four apostles, and of Mary. Each of these types of leaders reflects a different emphasis in the tradition of religious leadership. There is much that can be learned from each in their own right. We also learn by trying to see how these forms of leadership complement one another, for they all point us back to the type of leadership exercised by Jesus himself.

A second form of learning takes place by asking ourselves which is the most appropriate form of leadership for our situation. For the calls we pray about here also reflect the reality that each of us is called by God, and in that call we experience the drama of God's majesty, our own sinfulness, our fear of God as well as our own generosity and our ability to either resist or respond to God. Our struggle to hear the call of God in our work is reflected in the call of the heroes and prophets of the Old Testament, and their struggle to understand their role, and how they could have been chosen for it. In the stories of call in the New Testament, we can be inspired by the generosity of Mary's response and that of the apostles, and still we know how the apostles struggled to understand the implications of their call, and to remain faithful to it. All these stories reveal different responses to leadership roles in the history of salvation. They reveal and clarify for us aspects of our own call as teachers and school leaders.

And now the cry of the sons of Israel has come to
me, and I have witnessed the way in which the
Egyptians oppress them.

So come, I send you to Pharaoh to bring the sons
of Israel, my people, out of Egypt.

Moses said to God,
>   'Who am I to go to Pharaoh and bring the sons
>   of Israel out of Egypt?'

'I shall be with you' was the answer 'and this is the
sign by which you shall know that it is I who have
sent you... After you have led the people out of
Egypt, you will worship God on this mountain.'

Exodus 3:9-12

Moses said to Yahweh,
>   'Please, my Lord, I have never been eloquent,
>   even since you have spoken to your servant, for
>   I am slow and hesitant of speech.'

'Who gave a person a mouth?' Yahweh said to
him.
>   'Who makes a person dumb or deaf,
>   gives sight or makes blind?
>   Is it not I, Yahweh?
>   Now go, I shall help you speak
>   and instruct you what to say'

Exodus 4:10-12

> The cry of the sons of Israel has come to me, and
> I have witnessed the way in which the Egyptians
> have oppressed them.

The opening line of the passage points to God's sense of care for his people, and his desire to respond to their needs.

- What is the 'cry of the sons of Israel' at this particular time?
- How might God want to respond to that cry through education?
- Who are the Egyptians of today? In what way are people oppressed?
- What is the freedom offered by education?

Moses' response was one of reluctance – 'Who am I to go to Pharaoh?' This reluctance is reflected later, when Moses speaks to God about his lack of eloquence.

- What aspects of your role as teacher or leader make you reluctant?
- What about the role makes you nervous?
- How have you grown in appreciation of the importance of education for young people? What has been the development in your interest in helping other teachers grow in their understanding of the role of teaching?
- How has your role in helping others attain 'freedom' developed? What key events have clarified that role for you? Can you find a concrete instance when you have spoken the right word at the right time? What has helped you do this?
- How do you now see your role as leading others operate in the classroom or the school?

God promised Moses that He will be with him and that there would be signs for him – that the people would worship on the mountain, and that Moses would be helped to speak.

- What might these 'signs' stand for in the world of education?
  - People worshipping on the Holy Mountain
  - The leader being helped to speak

- When others look for signs and meaning of success in education, what do they typically look for? How are these the same, and how do they differ, from signs that God may be at work?
- What signs give you most encouragement What can you do to develop a deeper appreciation of these signs?

 THE CALL OF JEREMIAH

The word of Yahweh was addressed to me, saying
   'Before I formed you in the womb I knew you
   Before you came to birth I consecrated you
   I have appointed you as prophet to the nations'

I said 'Ah, Lord Yahweh; look, I do not know how to speak: I am a child.'

But Yahweh replied,
   'Do not say, I am a child
   Go now to those to whom I send you
   and say whatever I command you
   Do not be afraid of them,
   For I am with you to protect you
   It is Yahweh who speaks'.

Then Yahweh put out his hand and touch my mouth and said to me:
   'There! I am putting my words into your mouth.

LEADING LIFE TO THE FULL

Look, today I am setting you
over nations and over kingdoms
to tear up and to knock down
to destroy and to overthrow,
to build and to plant'.

Jeremiah 1:4-10

 ## *Reflection*

The opening words of this passage speak of God knowing Jeremiah and guiding him to the point where he becomes a 'prophet to the nations'.

- What are the key events in your life that led you to being a teacher and/or principal?
- Can you see any pattern, or providence, in these events?
- Is it possible to see these events as the clarification of a personal call?

Jeremiah showed some resistance to the call, saying 'I don't know how to speak. I am a child'.

- How is this true of your sense of being a Christian leader in the school or the classroom? Which areas of Christian leadership do you feel confident? In which areas do you feel less confident?
- What elements of your own journey to leadership have contributed to this balance?

God points out that he will be with Jeremiah, and will prompt him and protect him.

- Are there any times in your experience as a teacher or as a principal that you have happened to say the right thing at the right time, and had an unexpected influence on a situation you were dealing with?

- In what way can you cultivate the experience of 'knowing the right thing to say'?
- How can you cultivate the experience that God is with you, to protect you in difficult times?

The final part of the passage tells us how Jeremiah understood the call or role of prophet:

> Set over nations and kingdoms
> to tear up and to knock down
> to destroy and to overthrow
> to build and to plant

- Do you see any areas of your work which has a parallel in these four areas?
- Which area is the dominant aspect of your role as teacher/principal?
- In which of these roles are you most comfortable?

Applying the role of prophet to that of school leader.
- How do you understand the role of prophet in today's world?
- How does the leader as prophet differ from the leadership role displayed by Moses in the previous passage?
- In what way can the school principal be a prophet to each of the following: teachers, students, parents, wider community?
- In what way can the teacher be a prophet (a) among his/her colleagues, and (b) to the students?

He now went up into the hills and summoned
those he wanted.
So they came to him and he appointed twelve.
They were
  to be his companions,
  to be sent out to preach,
  with power to cast out devils.

Mark 3:13-15[2]

As he was walking by the Sea of Galilee he saw
two brothers, Simon, who was called Peter, and his
brother Andrew: they were making a cast in the
lake with their net, for they were fishermen.

And he said to them, 'Follow me and I will make
you fishers of men'.

And they left their nets at once and followed him.

Going on from there, he saw another pair of
brothers, James, son of Zebedee, and his brother
John; they were in their boat with their father
Zebedee, mending their nets, and he called them.

At once, leaving the boat and their father, they
followed him.

Matthew 4:18-22

Jesus summoned those he wanted to be his disciples.

- What do you think were the criteria Jesus used in selecting his disciples – academic ability, teaching skills, good interpersonal skills, personal holiness?
- What does Jesus' choice of disciples tell us about the important part of his mission?
- How does this apply to the mission of education today?

The disciples were to be companions of Jesus, sent out to preach and to cast out devils.

- What does each of these stand for in education today?
- How is the invitation to be a companion given to leaders, teachers, parents, students?
- How does the work of preaching take place in the school or classroom?
- What are the 'devils' that are cast out through teaching?

When Jesus invited Peter and Andrew, he told them he would make them 'fishers of men'.

- What image do you have for your work as a teacher or leader?
- What does this image reveal about your deepest desires for education?
- What is the common ground between your image and that used by Jesus with the apostles?
- How has God used your talents and interests to inspire you in your work?

The apostles are depicted as leaving everything to become disciples.

- What do you think was the attraction that allowed them do that?

- What is the main vision that makes your commitment to education worthwhile?
- What are the things that help you stay in touch with that vision?
- What are the things that distract you from that vision?

In the second passage, Jesus makes the distinction between disciples and apostles. The role of apostle was described as having three functions – to be a companion of Jesus, to preach and to cast out devils.

- What aspect of your work as teacher, principal or board member correspond to each of these aspects of apostleship?
- In which role do you think you achieve the most?
- In which activity are you most comfortable?
- In which activity do you feel most a Christian apostle?
- Which is the most difficult role for you?

 THE CALL OF MARY

> In the sixth month, the angel Gabriel was sent by God to a town in Galilee called Nazareth, to a virgin betrothed to a man named Joseph, of the House of David: and the Virgin's name was Mary.
>
> He went in and said to her,
> 'Rejoice, so highly favoured! The Lord is with you'.
>
> She was deeply disturbed by these words and asked herself what this greeting could mean.
>
> But the angel said to her,
> 'Mary, do not be afraid; you have won God's favour.

Listen! You are to bear a son, and you must name him Jesus.
He will be great and will be called Son of the Most High.
The Lord God will give him the throne of his ancestor David;
He will rule over the House of Jacob for ever and His reign will have no end.'

'But how will this come about, since I am a virgin?'

'The Holy Spirit will come upon you' the angel answered, 'and the power of the Most High will cover you with its shadow. And so the child will be holy, and will be called Son of God.

Know this too:
Your kinswoman Elizabeth has, in her old age, herself conceived a son, and she whom people called barren is now in her sixth month. For nothing is impossible to God'.

'I am the handmaid of the Lord', said Mary 'Let what you have said be done to me".

Luke 1:26-38

 ## **Reflection**

The angel tells Mary she is highly favoured.
- What was the root cause of this favour and the basis for her call?
- How does this compare with the 'call' to be a teacher or school principal?

In the calls we have seen up to now, there is a definite mission for the person called to do something, to be involved in some action. In Mary's situation, she was asked to facilitate God coming into the world. The action and glory was to be with God rather than Mary.

- Does this contrast have any parallels in the way we think about teaching, or school leadership?
- In what way is teaching or running a school like giving birth to and nurturing the 'Word of God'?
- What do you find attractive about this type of leadership?
- What in this type of leadership do you find difficult?

On receiving the call, Mary was afraid, and she wondered how this would come about.

- What was the source of Mary's fear?
- In what sense does a similar fear or puzzlement attach to teaching or running a school?
- How do you think the angel would reassure a teacher or school leader in a similar situation to Mary?

At the end of this passage, the angel says 'Your kinswoman Elizabeth has, in her old age, herself conceived a son...'

- In terms of the drama of God being present with humankind, what lessons can be drawn from comparing the stories of Mary and Elizabeth?
- Where was the greater drama taking place – in God's dealing with Mary or with Elizabeth?
- How did other people see the importance of the two pregnancies?
- What effect did the respective ages of Mary and Elizabeth have on other people's perception of events?
- How was the drama perceived later – at the birth of John the Baptist and of Jesus?

- What was it enabled some people to understand the real drama of what was happening, and others to miss the point?
- In the world of school, what are the dramatic events in which people find it easy to think of God being present?
- What are the events in which people might easily miss God present in their lives?
- What is it that prevents some people from seeing the presence of God in their lives?
- What do we learn about true leadership in the life of Mary?
- What are the things that distract us from this model of leadership?

Notes

1   Shakespeare, W. *Twelfth Night*. Act II, Scene V.
2   This same passage is to be found in Luke 6:12-16 and in Mt. 10:1-4 where it is followed by a fuller explanation of the work of being an apostle.

VISION IN CHRISTIAN LEADERSHIP

Vision

> Where there is no vision, the people perish
> (Proverbs 29:18)

Vision in scripture appears in two themes. The first relates to promise, which has a future orientation. This promise guides present action and helps the community interpret their present experience. The second theme is that of our ability to see God at work, which has a present-tense orientation. The focus here is often negative and relates to our blindness and our hardness of heart. Spiritual enlightenment involves the ability to see the vision and also to recognise the source of that vision.

Vision as promise
God's promise to humankind is central to the story of salvation. The promise can be seen in the Book of Genesis. In a simple form, God promised Noah that he would not visit destruction on humankind again, and gave the rainbow as a symbol of that promise. The story of God's initiative with the Chosen People developed when God invited Abraham to leave his home and promised that he would become a great nation, blessed among all others (Gen 12:1-7). These promises were

made to Abraham 'and his descendants, forever'. The promise was lived out as a covenant between God and the Israelites.

The promise was reiterated to key leaders such as Moses, who led the people out of slavery in Egypt. Here, the promise took on a very tangible form – possession of a Promised Land. During their wandering in the desert, the people constantly faced difficulties, and regretted leaving the fleshpots of Egypt. Moses reminded them of God's promise and it was this vision of the future that sustained them in the present, and moulded their identity as a nation.

When Israel was set up as a nation kingdom, this promise was renewed to David:

> Your house and your sovereignty will always stand secure before me and your throne will be established forever. (2 Sam 7:16)

This promise nourished the Israelites through the darkest hours of their history, as the kingdom split and was overrun by enemies. Despite their sinfulness, God's promise of faithfulness remained. He still looked after Israel, and his promise would be seen in the future Messiah, foretold by the prophets. His coming would help Israel reform and be faithful to their covenant with God.

> A shoot springs from the stock of Jesse
> A scion thrusts from his roots.
> On him the spirit of Yahweh rests
> A spirit of wisdom and insight
> A spirit of counsel and power
> A spirit of knowledge and fear of the Lord
> (Is 11:1-2)

The coming of the Messiah was to bring good times for those who believed. The Promised Land was to be a land 'flowing with milk and honey'. This vision reflected the idyllic nature of the Garden of Eden. More importantly, it was to be a time of justice.

> See, the days are coming – it is Yahweh who speaks
> When I will raise a virtuous branch for David
> Who will reign as true king and be wise
> Practising honesty and integrity in the land.
> (Jer 23:2)

In the New Testament, the promise of the Messiah was fulfilled in Jesus. The angel proclaimed at his conception:

> He will be great and will be called the Son of the Most High.
> The Lord God will give him the throne of his ancestor David.
> He will rule over the house of Jacob forever and his reign will have no end. (Luke 1:32-33)

At his baptism, the Spirit of God descended on Jesus like a dove and a voice proclaimed from heaven

> This is my Son, the Beloved; my favour rests on him. (Mt 3:17)

The vision that Jesus proclaimed in his work was that the Kingdom of God was at hand. The kingdom he preached was to have an effect in the present, and make the lives of others easier, by bringing peace and justice.

> The spirit of the Lord has been given to me,
> for he has anointed me.
> He has sent me to bring the good news to the poor,

to proclaim liberty to captives
and to the blind new sight;
to set the downtrodden free,
to proclaim the Lord's year of favour.
(Lk 4:18-19)

The kingdom also had a future promise. Jesus told parables where the Kingdom of God was seen as a feast, in which the Father shared his life and his love. The ability to enjoy the promise of the Kingdom of God was linked with how individuals acted on earth. The theme of judgement leading to the inheritance of the kingdom can be seen in the stories, among others, of Lazarus and Dives; the contrast between the wise and foolish virgins; the judgment scene where Jesus invites those who clothed the naked, fed the hungry and visited those in prison to join him in his kingdom, and condemns those who failed to recognise him in the needy to the fires of hell.

It is through Jesus that humankind has access to the Kingdom of God. He reveals the Father's promise in its fullness. He teaches the truth of the promise and gives witness to it in his faithfulness to the message. We experience this in a special way in the resurrection, where we see the promise of eternal life fulfilled in how Jesus conquered death. Jesus is 'the Way, the Truth and the Life' for us. We will reflect in greater depth on Jesus as a role model in theme six. At his ascension, he promised to be with us at all times and to send the Holy Spirit to continue his work. He maintained the sense of promise into the future, a promise that keeps the Church's hope alive.

I am going to prepare a place for you, and after I
have gone and prepared you a place, I shall return
to take you with me. (Jn.14:2-3)

The promise is good news, and is to be the focus of preaching in the early Church. The promise of the Messiah was universal, and the Israelites were to be the first to receive the offer of the Messiah's saving work. In Matthew, as Jesus sent out the disciples, he sent them first to the lost sheep of Israel (Mt. 10:6). In the early chapters of Acts, the message was preached first in Jerusalem and spread out to Israel, and later, through Paul, 'to all the gentiles'. The message held the tension between the present and the future. Hearing the message and responding to it was to have an effect on the lives of the faithful. There was also an anticipation that the Kingdom of God was immanent.

> At the trumpet of God, the voice of the archangel will call out the command and the Lord himself will come down from heaven; those who have died in Christ will be the first to rise, and then those of us who are still alive will be taken up in the clouds, together with them, to meet the Lord in the air. So we shall stay with the Lord forever. (1 Thes 4:16-17)

The vision is therefore something we look forward to. But the vision of Christianity is not the same vision as that of secular philosophers. The wisdom of Christianity includes a positive perspective on the Cross – on death, suffering and resurrection. The vision integrates all aspects of our experience, not just offering some future 'opium' to anaesthetise our current reality. Therefore, we are not spectators to this vision. We are called to participate in it. We are able to do so in so far as we ourselves are not blind to the vision. This leads to another perspective on vision – our own ability to see.

Vision as seeing
Three themes reflect on the ability of humankind to appreciate the vision of God's love and his work. The first of these themes

offers a contrast between light and darkness, the second deals with blindness and the third sees human stubbornness and hardness of heart as the cause of that blindness.

Light-darkness metaphors
In the creation story, God separated light from darkness on the first day. This forms the basis of a powerful symbolism used in scripture to portray the final destiny of humankind. Our final destiny is set out in terms of light and dark, life and death.

Light is a powerful symbol for God himself. In the Old Testament, the appearance of God is often associated with dazzling light, surrounded by fire or lightening in a storm. This symbolism was continued in the appearances of the Father at the baptism of Jesus and the Transfiguration. The light emphasises the majesty of God and the power of his presence. Yet, this presence is benevolent. It gives reassurance. It is a guiding light (Ps 18:19), leading the just so that

> Your light will rise in the darkness and your shadows become like noon. (Is 58:10)

However, the wicked man lives in darkness.

> We looked for light, all is darkness, for brightness and we walk in the dark. Like the blind we feel our way along walls and hesitate like men without eyes. We stumble as though noon were twilight and dwell in the dark like the dead. (Is 59:9-10)

Isaiah in particular links the promise of God with the theme of light:

> The people that walked in darkness has seen a great light; on those who live in a land of deep shadow a light has shone. (Is 9:1)

In the New Testament, Jesus develops the light-darkness theme in reflecting on his work.

> Whoever sees me, sees the one who sent me. I, the light, have come into the world, so that whoever believes in me need not stay in the dark anymore. (Jn 12:45-46)

Light is an important basis for discipleship. Peter proclaimed that God has called us 'out of the darkness into his wonderful light' (1Pet 2:9). In Matthew and in Luke, the life of the disciple is described in terms of a light, and they are encouraged to cultivate the light in their own life.

> No one lights a lamp and puts it in some hidden place or under a tub, but on the lamp-stand so that people may see the light when they come in. The lamp of your body is your eye. When your eye is sound, your whole body too is filled with light: but when it is diseased your body too will be all darkness. See to it then that the light inside you is not darkness. If, therefore, your whole body is filled with light, and no trace of darkness, it will be light entirely, as when the lamp shines on you with its rays'. (Lk 11:33-36)

For Paul, the challenge is to live in the light of God. He portrays the disciple as someone who not only lives in the light, but who has become light.

> You were darkness once, but now you are light in the Lord; be like children of light, for the effects of the light are seen in complete goodness and right

living and truth. Try to discover what the Lord
wants of you, having nothing to do with the futile
works of darkness but exposing them by contrast.
The things which are done in secret are things that
people are ashamed even to speak of; but anything
exposed by the light will be illuminated, and
anything illuminated turns into light. (Eph 5:8-14)

Matthew develops a number of images of the Kingdom of God
and how we grow in it. He claims that 'the virtuous will shine
like the sun in the kingdom of their Father' (Mt 13:43). The
Church still prays for her deceased members, 'May eternal light
shine upon them', and the preface for the mass of the dead
reflects that this new light will enable us to see differently, and
that we shall 'see God face to face' (Rev 22:4).

Blindness
Jesus' mission was to help people see. One of his most powerful
miracles was that of curing those who were blind. The
significance of this miracle is discussed in detail in the story of
the cure of the man born blind in John's gospel (chapter 9).
Significantly, the miracle takes place on the Sabbath, indicating
that Jesus was continuing the work of the Father (Jn 5:17).
Before the miracle takes place, Jesus points out its significance,
proclaiming that he is the light of the world (v.5). The story also
has many parallels with the story of Nicodemus (Jn 3:1-21)
where the cure of blindness can be compared with a new birth
through water and the Spirit. In fact, the cure is only finalised
through the ritual washing in the pool at Siloam.
    Blindness, as indeed were many infirmities in those days,
was linked to sin. The disciples asked Jesus, 'Rabbi, who sinned,
this man or his parents, for him to have been born blind?'. Jesus
points out that the real sin is not in being physically blind, but

in the blindness that refuses to acknowledge God at work. As the story unfolds, the man who was cured gradually comes to realise who Jesus is. At first, he simply recounts what Jesus has done: 'He put a paste on my eyes, and I washed, and I can see' (v.15). When questioned as to how this could be, he claimed that Jesus must be a prophet (v.17). When pressed, he claims he does not know anything about Jesus: 'I only know that I was blind and now I can see' (v.25) and later, in exasperation, he proclaims 'Ever since the world began it is unheard of for anyone to open the eyes of a man who was born blind; if this man were not from God, he couldn't do a thing' (vv.32-33). Later, when he meets Jesus, he believes in Him when Jesus tells him he is looking at the Son of Man.

The humility of the blind man contrasts with the faith of his parents and that of the Pharisees. His parents acknowledge the miracle, but do not look beyond that; 'We know he is our son and we know he was born blind but we don't know how it is that he can see now, or who opened his eyes. He is old enough: let him speak for himself' (9:20-21). The Pharisees are more antagonistic. They complain that Jesus worked the miracle on the Sabbath. They assert that Jesus is a sinner. When challenged by the blind man, they refuse to acknowledge that God could be speaking through Jesus, as they know God through Moses. They drive the man away. When challenged by Jesus, they claim that they are not blind, and Jesus replies:

> Blind? If you were, you would not be guilty, but
> since you say, 'We see', your guilt remains. (9:41)

The presence of Jesus therefore has two effects. He gives sight to the man who was born blind. However, his presence as the light also blinds those who rely on their own sight and claim not to be blind.

It is for judgement that I have come into this
world, so that those without sight may see and
those with sight turn blind. (9:39)

Hardness of heart

The underlying distinction between physical and spiritual
blindness is the disposition of the person's heart. Hardness of
heart characterises the state of the sinner who refuses to be
converted and remains separated from God. The heart is the
centre of love, and any coarseness in the heart prevents the
person from seeing the vision of God or from hearing his word
properly. Just as men 'preferred darkness to the light because
their deeds were evil' (Jn 3:19), so also hardness of heart
prevented Pharaoh from understanding the signs worked by
Moses (Ex 7-11) and caused the Israelites to complain about
Yahweh in the desert despite the earlier miracles leading to the
Exodus (Num 14:11). In the New Testament, especially in
John's gospel, we find the people constantly asking Jesus for
signs to show who he is. He works miracles for them, and
although they see the miracles, they still do not believe. Jesus
described the generation:

> For John came, neither eating nor drinking, and
> they say, 'He is possessed'. The Son of Man came,
> eating and drinking, and they say, 'Look, a glutton
> and a drunkard, a friend of tax collectors and
> sinners'. (Mt 11:18-19)

After the miracle of the loaves, Jesus met closed minds of those
who had not seen the meaning of the miracle (Mk 6:52, 8:17-
18) and John tells us that many disciples left him after this
miracle (Jn 6:66). The people saw the miracle, but their
hardness of heart prevented them from understanding it. Jesus
lamented this.

The reason I talk to them in parables is that they look without seeing and listen without hearing or understanding. So in their cases this prophecy of Isaiah is being fulfilled:

You will listen and listen again, but not understand,
See and see again, but not perceive.

For the heart of this nation has grown coarse, their ears are dull of hearing, and they have shut their eyes, for fear they should see with their eyes, hear with their ears, understand with their heart, and be converted and be healed by me. (Mt 12:13-15, quoting Is 6:9-10)

In that context, much of the preaching of the disciples was for repentance – helping people to recognise their past blindness and hardness of heart. John the Baptist preached 'Repent, for the kingdom of heaven is close at hand' (Mt 3:2). In the early Church, each of the apostolic discourses ended with a call to repentance: 'Now you must repent and turn to God so that your sins may be wiped out' (Acts 3:19). This conversion, or metanoia, means a turning away from past (the darkness) and embracing the future (the light).

Many of the examples of hardness of heart in the gospels are related to those in leadership positions. Jesus constantly pointed out the hypocrisy of the leaders of the day; men who sought honour for themselves by their attention to detail; who twisted the law to suit themselves; who placed burdens on others but never helped them; who preached one thing and did another.

They are blind men leading blind men; and if one blind man leads another, both will fall into a pit.
(Mt 15:14)

The call to leadership therefore involved a call to personal conversion and authentic living before making any demands on others.

> Hypocrite! Take the plank out of your own eye
> first, and then you will see clearly enough to take
> the splinter out of your brother's eye. (Mt 7:5)

Vision in education today

The theme of vision is easily applied to modern developments in educational leadership. Schools are expected to develop vision statements and mission statements that express their dreams for the future. The key role of any leader is to help the school be in touch with that vision and appreciate its application. In developing the vision of a Catholic school it is important to be in touch with true gospel values and not distort them according to our own prejudices. Thus, the vision dimension of leadership involves clarifying the promise contained in the vision and also helping others (including ourselves) be healed of our blindness and hardness of heart.

For the teacher in the classroom a key outcome is that students develop a vision of themselves, the world around them and the contribution they can make to that world. The teacher may introduce the students to elements of the content of that vision and help them explore its richness through the perspectives of language, literature, science, history, art and the applied subjects. Exposure to different ways of seeing the world hopefully removes blindness and prejudice, freeing the students to continue to explore and appreciate God's creation and to respond to the call to contribute to the world in which they live.

In this section we explore four scripture passages related to vision. The first is from the Old Testament and examines the vision of human fulfilment as life or death. The second passage reflects on Jesus' own mission statement from the synagogue in Nazareth – a mission that we might share. The third passage describes Paul's vision of the human person and their development. The fourth places that vision in the context of secular vision and reflects on what might be called the countercultural nature of Christian vision.

 ## CHOOSING LIFE OVER DEATH

For this Law that I enjoin on you today is not
beyond your strength or beyond your reach.
It is not in heaven, so that you need to wonder
'Who will go up to heaven for us and bring it
down to us, so that we may hear it and keep it?"
Nor is it beyond the seas, so that you need to
wonder, 'Who will cross the seas for us and bring
it back to us, so that we may hear it and keep?'
No, the Word is very near to you.
It is in your mouth and in your heart for your
observance.

See, today, I set before you life and prosperity,
death and disaster.

If you obey the commandments of Yahweh your
God that I enjoin on you today,
If you love Yahweh your God and follow his
ways,
if you keep his commandments, his laws, his
customs,
you will live and increase,
and Yahweh your God will bless you
in the land which you are entering to make
your own.

But if your heart strays,
   if you refuse to listen,
   if you let yourself be drawn into worshipping
   other gods
   and serving them,
I tell you today, you will most certainly perish,
   you will not live long in the land you are
   crossing the Jordan to enter and possess.
I call heaven and earth to witness against you
   today:

I set before you life or death, blessing or curse.
Choose life, then so that you and your descendants
   may live in the love of Yahweh your God,
   obeying his voice, clinging to him.
For in this your life consists,
   and on this depends your long stay in the land
   which
   Yahweh swore to your fathers Abraham, Isaac
   and Jacob he would give them.

Deuteronomy 30:9-20

 ## *Reflection*

The first part of this passage states that the Word is very near –
it is in our mouth and in our heart for our observance.

- What are the implications of this belief for education?
- How do we promote this belief
  - in our dealings with students?
  - in motivating their academic work?

- in relationships with them in classroom?
- in our relationship with colleagues?
- in partnerships with parents?
- What aspects of school life make this belief difficult in each of the areas mentioned above?

In the passage, the acceptance of the Law is seen as a choice between life and prosperity *or* death and disaster.
- How convinced are you that education offers a young person a similar choice between life and death, prosperity and disaster? What might 'life and death', 'prosperity and disaster' look like in this context?
- To what extent do you believe that people can actually *choose* life or death, prosperity or disaster, in the sense that this passage intimates? What things block young people from making 'life' choices? What entices them to choose 'death' in their decisions?
- In what we offer young people in schools, what aspects of school life can be seen as 'life and prosperity'? What aspects might they see as 'death and disaster'? What do you do as a teacher or leader to help a young person see the choice and opt for life and prosperity?
- How do you see your role as a teacher or a school leader in helping others make such a choice? Can you celebrate experiences in which you have helped others choose and find 'life and prosperity'? Are there occasions when some chose 'death and disaster'? How did you respond to these situations? How might these experiences speak to you about your calling as a teacher?
- How much do you see teaching or school leadership as your choice for life and prosperity? What aspects of your experience of teaching affirm this for you? In what way do you experience teaching as 'death and disaster'?

Jesus, with the power of the Spirit in him, returned to Galilee: and his reputation spread through the countryside. He taught in their synagogues and everyone praised him.

He came to Nazara, where he had been brought up, and went into the synagogue on the Sabbath day as he usually did.

He stood up to read, and they handed him the scroll of the prophet Isaiah. Unrolling the scroll he found the place where it is written:

> The spirit of the Lord has been given to me,
> for he has anointed me.
> He has sent me to bring the good news to the poor,
> to proclaim liberty to captives
> and to the blind new sight;
> to set the downtrodden free,
> to proclaim the Lord's year of favour.

He then rolled up the scroll, gave it back to the assistant and sat down. And all eyes in the synagogue were fixed on him.

Then he began to speak to them,

'This text is being fulfilled today even as you listen.'

Luke 4:14-21

Reflection

- What does this passage tell us about the source of Jesus' sense of mission?
- What key events might have led Jesus to this sense of mission?
- Jesus quotes five areas in which he sees his mission being fulfilled? Can you give examples of how this was lived out in practice in his own life?
- How would you characterise the effect of each of these five practices on Jesus' followers?

Now, apply some of what you have considered above to your own work as a teacher or leader.

- In what way do you consider your work as sharing Jesus' sense of mission?
- How have you come to realise that sense of mission?
- What practices of teaching or school leadership correspond to the five areas quoted by Jesus:
  - bringing good news to the poor?
  - proclaiming liberty to captives?
  - giving the blind new sight?
  - setting the downtrodden free?
  - proclaiming the Lord's favour?
- How does good teaching and leadership bring about the effect Jesus wished to have on his followers?
- What can you do to stay in touch with your sense of Christian mission in teaching and education? How do you try to maintain the balance between the five different aspects of the mission? What supports do you have? How well do you feel you use these supports?

PAUL'S PRAYER FOR CHRISTIAN FULFILMENT

This then is what I pray, kneeling before the Father, from whom every family, whether spiritual or natural, takes its name:

Out of his infinite glory, may he give you the power through his Spirit for your hidden self to grow strong, so that Christ may live in your hearts through faith, and then, planted in love and built on love, you will with all the saints have strength to grasp the breadth and the length, the height and the depth; until, knowing the love of Christ, which is beyond all knowledge, you are filled with the utter fullness of God.

Glory be to him whose power, working in us, can do infinitely more than we can ask or imagine; glory be to him from generation to generation in the Church and in Christ Jesus for ever and ever. Amen.

Ephesians 3:14-21

 Reflection

- How can this prayer 'that your hidden self grow strong' be addressed in the school context -
    - for those in leadership positions?
    - for teachers and other staff?
    - for students?
    - for parents?

- What does the context of 'planted in love and built on love' stand for in the school? How does your school promote this atmosphere? What factors challenge that context?
- How do you move beyond 'grasping the breadth and the length, the height and the depth' to 'knowing the love of Christ' and being 'filled with the utter fullness of God'?
- What sense of affirmation do you have in your role as a Christian educator?
- How do you help teachers experience this affirmation themselves?
- How do you understand this concept for the student and the parent?

 ## PAUL'S VISION OF WISDOM

Christ did not send me to baptise,
    but to preach the Good News,
and not to preach that in the terms of philosophy
    in which the crucifixion of Christ cannot be
    expressed.

The language of the cross may be illogical to those who are not on the way to salvation, but those of us who are on the way see it as God's power to save.

As scripture says:
    I shall destroy the wisdom of the wise
    and bring to nothing all the learning of the
    learned.

Where are the philosophers now?
Where are the scribes?
Where are any of our thinkers today?
Do you see now how God has shown up the foolishness of human wisdom?

If it was God's wisdom that human wisdom
should not know God,
it was because God wanted to save those who have
faith
through the foolishness of the message that we
preach.

And so, while the Jews demand miracles
and the Greeks look for wisdom,
here are we preaching a crucified Christ:

to the Jews an obstacle that they cannot get over,
to the pagans madness,
but to those who have been called, whether they
are Jews or Greeks,
a Christ who is the power and the wisdom of God.

For God's foolishness is wiser than human wisdom,
and God's weakness is stronger than human
strength.

                          1 Corinthians 1:17-25

 ## *Reflection*

- How do we value the 'wisdom of philosophers' in school today?
- What does the 'foolishness of Christ crucified' stand for in the school setting? In what way is this valued?
- Are these two types of wisdom necessarily at odds with one another?
- In what way can we distort one over the other? Which type of wisdom is typically underdeveloped in school? Why do you think this is?

                                        LEADING LIFE TO THE FULL

- In what way are the values of Christian education counter-cultural – an obstacle that cannot be surmounted, or regarded as sheer madness? How strong are the cultural forces that work against these values in the school? What are the 'miracles' and the 'wisdom' that students, parents and society look for from education? How does the school cope with this tension?
- How do you experience this tension between values in your work – in a leadership position or in the classroom? How do you cope with the tension? What would the ideal be in resolving this tension? How do you stay in touch with the Christian vision?
- How many students attain the wisdom of philosophers to a high level? What happens to those who do not succeed? What are the main requirements for success in this area?
- What are the requirements for attaining the wisdom of Christ? What leads to that wisdom? To how many students is that wisdom open? How is it recognised and celebrated: (a) in the school? (b) in the classroom?

THEME 3

LEADERSHIP STYLES

In the section on spirituality and leaders, we noted the use of archetypes to describe different types of leaders and applied this to developing the idea of the hero in leadership. In the introduction to Theme 1, 'The Call to Leadership', we noted how different forms of leadership emerged in Israel, giving rise to three different archetypes – priest, king and prophet. Jesus fulfilled each of these archetypes in his ministry. Each Christian, by way of baptism, also shares in these archetypes. In this theme we focus once more on these archetypes. We also add a fourth, that of servant. Jesus characterised Christian leadership as one of service.

Priest

In the early history of Israel, there were no official priests. The patriarchs built their own altars and offered their own sacrifice, as is evident in the story of Abraham offering his son as a sacrifice. It is only with Moses that the priesthood took on an official function and became institutionalised in the tribe of Levi. Moses described the work of the priest as follows:

> They have kept your word, they hold firmly to
> your covenant. They teach your customs to Jacob,

your Law to Israel. They send incense rising to your nostrils, place the holocaust on your altar. (Dt 33:9-11)

With the monarchy, the priesthood was centred in the temple of Jerusalem, the centre of Israel's worship. There was a high priest and a number of other officials based in the temple, and other members of the priestly caste officiated in the various sanctuaries around the kingdom. The king protected the priests, and indeed he carried out a number of priestly functions. For instance, David offered sacrifice of an ox and a sheep when the ark of the covenant was brought to Jerusalem. When the ark was brought to the temple for the first time, 'the king turned and blessed the whole assembly of Israel, while the whole assembly of Israel stood' (1K 8:15)

It is only with the ruin of the temple and the monarchy that priesthood emerged as a powerful role in Israel. They become the spiritual guides of the people, with two main functions. The first of these was the office of worship. The priest presided over the liturgies at the time of feasts. At a liturgy of sacrifice, he acted as a mediator between God and the people, presenting their offering. The priest was also in charge of the rites of consecration and purification. Lepers were told to present themselves to the priests to show they had been cured (Mt 8:4), and women were also to be purified after delivering children (Luke 2:22). The second function was related to tradition. The tradition was recalled in the memories of the past and in the Law. In the liturgy, the priests recounted the narratives. A central aspect of this narrative is the covenant, particularly as exemplified in the Law. The priests were the guardians of the Law. They copied it in the holy books and interpreted its meaning for the people.

The role of priest therefore is to mediate something of the sacred meaning of events to others. This can be done by managing symbolism, through ritual and story telling. Symbols are very important elements in the way we proclaim our identity and in how we integrate new events into our understanding of life.

King

In many ancient civilisations, the king was regarded as a God. This was certainly true of Pharaoh. He acted as a mediator between the gods and man. He was responsible for justice, victory and peace. Through him, all blessings came, including the fertility of the crops. However, for the Israelites, the king was never divine, as there was only one God. The kingship was a temporal institution, set up in the face of attacks from the Philistines. The idea was borrowed from their neighbours:

> We want a king, so that we in our turn can be like
> the other nations; our king shall rule us and be our
> leader and fight our battles. (1Sam 8:19-20)

However, the king was subject to the Law, and could not rise above it. Yet, the fact that he was consecrated by Yahweh gave him special prominence. God made the king his adopted son and promised him protection. By victories over external enemies he assured the prosperity of the people. By victories over internal enemies, he assured justice and peace.

Bad kings were numerous and the kings constantly gave in to the temptation of aligning themselves with the example of the pagan monarchies. They imitated their despotism and made themselves gods. They were constantly denounced by the prophets. Their lack of repentance eventually led to the fall and exile of Israel.

Within the kingdom, the main function of the king was related to justice. He was the final arbiter of disputes. Many of

LEADING LIFE TO THE FULL

the stories about Solomon's wisdom in adjudicating between people are well known. In contrast with the role of the priest, the role of the king dealt with secular issues, although in the mind of the Israelites, the law of justice was intimately connected with the religious experience of the covenant.

Prophet

In ancient tribes, there was always someone who acted as a mediator between God and man. People came to him to find out what lay in store for them, or what God (or the gods) wanted of them. The prophet discerned this through divination or magic.

For the Israelites, Moses was the first prophet. He heard the word of God and transmitted it to the people. In the later development of the role, all the great prophets – Samuel, Elijah, Isaiah, Jeremiah, Ezekiel – were animated by the spirit of God. It was from God that they got their message. Their role was that of revealing God's message to the community, helping them to discover what they could not by their own efforts.

Thus, the role of prophet had a very different source to that of the priest and king. These latter roles were inherited. The role of the prophet was not. As we saw in Theme 1, the prophet was individually called by God. In Israel, prophet was a distinct role from that of priest and king, and sometimes these roles were in conflict. Frequently, the prophet acted as an advisor to the king. Nathan, Isaiah and Jeremiah all acted as advisors but were not afraid to criticise the monarch if they thought that actions taken did not correspond with God's wishes, or where a policy was unjust and did not fit into the pattern of salvation. The prophecy frequently began 'Yahweh says this'.

Rather than predicting the future, the prophet was therefore a commentator on the life of the state, pointing to the religious meaning in everyday events. However, the message was often accompanied by some symbolic action. Jeremiah purchased a field (32), Hosea used the image of the unfaithful wife, and Ezekiel reflected on the meaning of illness and mental anguish (Ezekiel 3:25, 4:4-8) .

Sometimes, the prophet acted with the priest, especially in the coronation of the king. However, the prophets were acutely aware of the danger of cultic practices becoming sacrilegious.

> I hate and despise your feasts. I take no pleasure in your solemn festivals. When you offer me holocausts, I reject your oblations, and refuse to look at your sacrifices of fattened cattle. Let me have no more of the din of your chanting, no more of your strumming on harps. But let justice flow like water and integrity like an unfailing stream. (Amos 5:21-24)

The key element for the prophet was to ensure that the meaning that was celebrated in symbolic and cultic practice translated to an authentic lifestyle.

> Yet here you are, trusting in delusive words, to no purpose! Steal, would you, murder, commit adultery, perjure yourselves, burn incense to Baal, follow alien gods that you do not know? – and then come presenting yourselves in this Temple that bears my name, saying; Now we are safe – safe to go on committing these abominations! (Jer 7:8-10)

The prophet interpreted the present and held a mirror to the people so that they could see their actions in the light of God's word to them. Although the focus was on the present, there was also a future perspective. The prophet frequently called the community to repentance, and pointed out the consequences of their actions to them.

Three archetypes applied to school

In any school setting, there is the role of king, which organises, sets rules and disciplines. There is also the priestly role, which explains and interprets the syllabus to students. But these roles are balanced by the role of the prophet, who develops a critical reflection linking theory and practice. Teachers in classrooms are often called on to play all three roles – classroom management (king), explaining and interpreting the lesson (priest) and developing critical reflective approaches in the student through their curiosity and experimentation (prophet). School leaders also play these same roles in the running of schools. There is the managerial aspect of their work, ensuring that the school runs in a smooth and just manner (king). They are also stewards of a vision of education, ensuring that values are interpreted correctly (priest). They also reflect on the direction of the school into the future, and its response to the needs of students, parents and teachers. As they plan for the future, they not only want to do things right, they also want to do the right thing. This is the role of the prophet.

The three archetypes of king, priest and prophet are well embedded in the Old Testament. In the New Testament, Jesus exemplifies each of these roles. More importantly for us, however, is that each of us is anointed as priest, prophet and king at our baptism. These roles are not special functions embedded in appointments in school. They belong to each of us as Christians. Part of our Christian formation is to understand what the roles mean in our present culture. It is in the expression of these roles that each individual in the school community has an opportunity to become a closer follower of the gospel vision. In this way, we build up a community of leaders in our schools.

A key to understanding how this works is to reflect on an archetype developed in a special way in the New Testament. Jesus told his disciples that their leadership was to be a leadership of service. The service is not the service of a slave, but that of an adopted child. Hearing the word of God changes a person. They are no longer slaves to sin, but experience the freedom of the children of God. We read how this lead the apostles to the service of the word they saw in Jesus and heard from him.

> Something which has existed since the beginning,
> that we have heard, and we have seen with our own
> eyes; that we have watched and touched with our
> hands: the Word, who is life – this is our subject.
> (1 Jn 1:1)

Servant
When Zebedee's wife approached Jesus, looking for a favoured place for her two sons when Jesus came into his kingdom, Jesus spoke to his disciples about the ideal of service in leadership.

> Among pagans it is the kings who lord it over
> them, and those who have authority over them are
> given the title Benefactor. This must not happen
> with you. No; the greatest among you must
> behave as if were the youngest, the leader as if he
> were the one who serves. For who is the greater;
> the one at table or the one who serves? The one at
> table, surely? Yet here am I among you as one who
> serves! (Luke 22:25-27)

He exemplified this service himself at the Last Supper, when he washed the feet of the disciples.

> If I, then, the Lord and Master, have washed your feet, you should wash each other's feet. I have given you an example so that you may copy what I have done to you. I tell you most solemnly, no servant is greater than his master, no messenger is greater than the man who sent him. (Jn 13:14-16)

Jesus' service is given in the context of his own mission from the Father. From an early age, he was conscious that 'I must be about my Father's business' (Lk 2:49).

> The world must be brought to know that I love the Father and that I am doing exactly what the Father told me. (Jn 14:30)

Jesus identifies faithful service to the word of God as the keynote of discipleship:

> Stretching out his hand towards his disciples he said, 'Here are my mother and my brothers. Anyone who does the will of my Father in heaven, he is my brother and sister and mother'.
> (Mt 12:48-49)

The theme of service is to be seen in other metaphors used by Jesus in the New Testament. The principal metaphor is that of shepherd, an image that was developed in the Old Testament ('Yahweh is my Shepherd', Ps. 23). This imagery is continued to describe Jesus' work. In his early ministry he looked at the crowd and took pity on them, because 'they were like sheep without a shepherd' (Mk 6:34). He used the shepherd who leaves ninety-nine sheep to seek out one that is lost as a metaphor of God's love for the sinner. In sending out the disciples for the first time, he sent them to the 'lost sheep of Israel' (Mt 10:6). He recognised that this flock would be attacked by external enemies, so that the disciples were to be 'like sheep among wolves' and must be as 'cunning as serpents and yet as harmless as doves' (Mt 10:16). They would also be attacked internally by 'false prophets who come to you disguised as sheep but underneath are ravenous wolves' (Mt 7:15). This theme is developed in detail in chapter 10 of John's gospel. Jesus is the good shepherd. He cares for his sheep and knows each one, and they recognise him. He also guards access to the sheep (as the gate of the sheepfold) and gives authority to others to guide the sheep. Enemies come to attack and scatter the sheep. The hope is that there will be only one flock and one shepherd, and the exemplar of service is that Jesus lays down his life for his sheep.

This service is all embracing. But there are many distractions to serving God. Chief among them is the lure of riches. Attachment to riches entices people to seek their own short-term comfort rather than answering the call of service. A condition for following Jesus is a rejection of riches and a focus on service.

> No one can be the slave of two masters: he will either hate the first and love the second, or treat the first with respect and the second with scorn. You cannot be the slave both of God and of money. (Mt 6:24)

As well as portraying an ideal of leadership, Jesus was very critical of the leadership he saw in his day. He contrasted the inadequacy of human leaders and their concern for their followers with God's love for his people. One example of this was the widow who appealed to the judge for justice, but got no response. Finally, he gave in, not out of any sense of justice, but simply to get rid of her.

In Matthew's gospel (18:1-10), Jesus had very strong words for those who led others astray. The context here focuses on innocent children, but can also be extended to all followers of Jesus, who were encouraged to become like these children.

> Alas for the world that there should be such
> obstacles! Obstacles indeed there must be, but alas
> for the man who provides them! (Mt 18:7)

In two of the gospels we are told that at the beginning of his ministry, Jesus himself was tempted to take on a different type of leadership (Mt 4 and Mk 1). The devil tempts him to become a material messiah (turning stones into bread), then a political messiah with the accompanying power (throwing himself off the parapet) and wealth (owning the kingdoms seen from the top of the mountain). However, Jesus resisted these temptations for a leadership of obedience to the will of God and service.

> You must worship the Lord your God and serve
> him alone. (Mt 4:10, Dt. 6:13)

Hearing the word of God and accepting it changes people. They move, through baptism, from a bondage in sin to a friendship with God (Rom 6:4). They are called children of God and share the inheritance of the Son (Gal 4:1-11). The service given by the Christian therefore is the service of a child of God, not that of a slave.

> I tell you most solemnly, everyone who commits
> sin is a slave. Now the slave's place in the house is
> not assured, but the son's place is assured. So if the
> Son makes you free, you will be free indeed.
> (Jn 8:34-35)

Paul realised that there was a variety of gifts that could be put at the service of the Christian community. He recognised that these gifts all came from the one Spirit, and that therefore, the leadership of the community was a team effort. He used the analogy of the body, where different gifts were seen as different parts of the body, each contributing to the life of the body (1 Cor 12:12-30). He goes on to outline the relative importance of different spiritual gifts, underlining the essential quality of love for the service of others (1 Cor 13-14). The focus here is on the essential purpose of leadership – to promote the unity of all Christians in the Church, which is the Body of Christ.

Reflections

The scripture passages in this section focus mainly on the service ideal in leadership. It might be useful to return to Theme 1 on the call of the leadership and reflect on some of the passages again, but this time from the perspective of leadership style. You can do this by asking questions of yourself such as how this call might be seen in practice.

The first passage chosen here is from the Letter of Peter. It focuses on leadership as inspired by a vision and at the service of others. The second passage from Matthew's gospel reflects on the ideal of service in leadership. The third passage, from the first letter to the Corinthians, explores the idea of the leadership team, where each person uses their gifts in the service of the vision. The story of the disciples on the road to Emmaus shows Jesus in a leadership role where he helped the disciples see the core meaning of events and be affirmed in their following of the vision. The final passage in this section looks at the temptations of Jesus in the desert as a contrast between Christian and secular leadership.

Now I have something to tell your elders:

I am an elder myself, and a witness to the
sufferings of Christ,
And with you I have a share in the glory that is to
be revealed.

Be the shepherds of the flock of God that is
entrusted to you:
    Watch over it, not simply as a duty, but gladly,
    because God wants it.
    Not for sordid money, but because you are
    eager to do it.
    Never be a dictator over any group that is put in
    your charge,
    But be an example that the whole flock can
    follow.

When the chief shepherd appears, you will be
given the crown of unfading glory.

First Letter of Peter 5:1-4

 Reflection

In the first verse, Peter reflects on his call to be an elder, or
leader, in the community. In it, he links his past experience to
his sense of present call; he sees himself as being a leader, but
also a follower in the sense that he is a witness to Christ; he is
aware of both suffering and glory in his experience.

In your experience of being an 'elder' or leader in the school community,

- How do you see your past experience influencing your present sense of what it is to be a leader?
- How do you balance your own sense of discipleship and witness to your sense of leading and influencing other people?
- What are the sufferings and glory that make up your experience of being an elder?

In the next two verses, Peter speaks of a style of leadership. In each case, he contrasts two different perspectives on leadership, and promotes one of these as being the more appropriate Christian response.

- How do you experience leadership as 'a sense of duty' and as 'a willing response'?
- How do you balance these demands in your own style?
- What motivates you in your work? What are the extrinsic motivators? What are the intrinsic motivators?
- How do you maintain a positive balance between these forces?
- How do you experience the issues of 'power and authority' and 'role modelling and service' in your work?
- How do you balance these aspects of your work?

In the final verse, Peter speaks of his hopes of 'a crown of unfading glory'.

- What do you hope for in your relationship with God through the role you play?

Then the mother of Zebedee's sons came with her
sons to make a request of him, and bowed low;

And he said to her
  'What is it you want?"

She said to him,
'Promise that these two sons of mine may sit one
at your right hand and the other at your left in
your kingdom'.

'You do not know what you are asking' Jesus
answered.
  'Can you drink the cup that I am going to drink?'

They replied, 'We can'.

'Very well', he said 'You shall drink my cup,
    but as for seats at my right hand and my left,
    these are not mine to grant;
    they belong to those to whom they have been
    allotted by my Father'.

When the other ten heard this they were indignant
with the two brothers.
But Jesus called them to him and said

'You know that among the pagans the rulers lord it
over them,
    and their great men make their authority felt.
    This is not to happen among you.

No: anyone who wants to be great among you
must be your servant,

and anyone who wants to be first among you must be your slave, just as the Son of Man came not to be served, but to serve, and to give his life as a ransom for many.

Matt 20:20-28

 ## *Reflection*

- What did the mother of the disciples hope for her sons?
- What were the disciples hoping for when they came with her?
- What did they expect of a leadership position with Jesus?
- What was your expectation of a leadership role in education – either as a teacher or a leader?
- How did Jesus respond to the disciples?
- What did he think of their request?
- In his reply, what did he focus on?
- What do you see as the link between the practice of leadership and the recognition of good leadership by others?
- What is your expectation of others who might be good leaders?
- What do other people expect of you in your leadership roles?
- Jesus takes the opportunity to teach his disciples about servant leadership?
- What is the focus of the leader's service?
- What vision inspires that service?
- Is this kind of leadership possible, or desirable, in schools?
- Have you any images of someone who acted in this way towards you?
- What type of 'service' do you appreciate from leaders?
- Are there times when you have given this type of leadership to others?

- How have 'followers' responded to that type of leadership?
- What effect has the experience of being this type of leader had on you?
- How does the servant leadership spoken of here by Jesus differ from a leadership style that allows others take advantage of you?
- What are key elements of the leader-follower relationship with servant leadership? How do you prepare for this type of relationship?

 ## LEADERSHIP AS A TEAM

> There is a variety of gifts but always the same Spirit: there are all sorts of service to be done, but always to the same Lord: working in all sorts of different ways in different people, it is the same God who is working an all of them. The particular way in which the Spirit is given to each person is for a good purpose. One may have the gift of preaching with wisdom given him by the Spirit; another may have the gift of preaching instruction given him by the same Spirit; and another the gift of faith given by the same Spirit; another again the gift of healing, through this one Spirit; one, the power of miracles; another, prophecy; another the gift of recognising spirits; another the gift of tongues and another the ability to interpret them. All these are the work of one and the same Spirit, who distributes different gifts to different people just as he chooses.
>
> *1 Corinthians 12:4-11*

Reflection

Take a few moments to read and reflect on the passage above.

- What do you think Paul's purpose is in asking the Christians at Corinth to reflect on the different gifts in the community?
- How do you think this purpose might apply in a school?
- List the nine gifts mentioned by St Paul. How might each of these gifts apply to the work of education and schooling?
- In what way do you think these gifts apply to you in your work as a leader? What gifts do you feel called on to use? What gifts are you comfortable with? What gifts are you not comfortable with?
- In what way do you see these gifts in other people in your school? Can you see how each of the gifts is promoted in the school? Can you look at different members of the staff and see one or more of these gifts in them?
- If these gifts are connected with the fullness of leadership, and the gifts are distributed among different people, what are the implications for the way in which you exercise leadership in the school?

 ## THE DISCIPLES ON THE ROAD TO EMMAUS

Two of the disciples were on their way to a village called Emmaus, seven miles from Jerusalem. They were talking together about all that had happened. Now, as they talked this over, Jesus himself came up and walked by their side, but something prevented them from recognising him. He said to them, 'What matters are you discussing as you walk along?' They stopped short, their faces downcast.

One of them, called Cleopas, answered him, 'You must be the only person staying in Jerusalem who does not know the things that have been happening there these last few days'. 'What things?' he asked. 'All about Jesus of Nazareth' they answered 'who proved he was a great prophet by the things he said and did in the sight of God and of the whole people; and how our chief priests and our leaders handed him over to be sentenced to death, and had him crucified. Our own hope had been that he would be the one to set Israel free.

And this is not all: two whole days have gone by since it all happened; and some women from our group have astounded us: they went to the tomb in the early morning and when they did not find the body, they came back to tell us they had seen a vision of angels who declared he was alive. Some of our friends went to the tomb and found everything exactly as the women had reported, but of him they saw nothing'.

Then he said to them 'You foolish men! So slow to believe the full message of the prophets! Was it not ordained that the Christ should suffer and so enter into his glory? Then, starting with Moses and going through all the prophets, he explained to them the passages throughout the scriptures that were about himself.

When they drew near to the village to which they were going, he made as if to go on; but they pressed him to stay with them. 'It is nearly evening' they said 'and the day is almost over'. So he went in to stay with them. Now, while he was with them at table, he took the bread and said the blessing: then he broke it and handed it to them. And their eyes were opened and they recognised him; but he had vanished from their sight. They they said to each other, 'Did not our hearts burn within us as he talked to us on the road and explained the scriptures to us?'

Luke 24: 13-32

 ## *Reflection 1*

Personal

'What matters are you discussing as you walk along?'
They stopped short, their faces downcast.

• How does this apply to you? Who do you 'walk along the road with', talking about matters relating to school? What matters do you discuss which make you downcast? When others want to walk with you, what matters do they want to discuss?

Our own hope had been that he would be the one to set Israel free.

• When you talk about disappointments, are there people (e.g. our chief priests and leaders) you think are responsible for this frustration? Where do you direct your frustration? If,

LEADING LIFE TO THE FULL

instead of focusing on the frustration, you were to express the dream in a positive way, what would your hope be?

> Some women from our group have astounded us....
> They had seen a vision of angels who declared he was alive

- Who are the people who challenge you to look at your work in a different way? What are the main areas of your work that you find 'deadening' and need to be 'enlivened'? How do you find out about these areas?

> He explained to them the passages that were about himself.

- Who or what are the main sources of inspiration for you in your work? Who helps you make connections with the bigger picture? Who helps you see your work in terms of Catholic education? Personal christian development?

> Did not our hearts burn within us as he talked to us on the road...

- What about your work gives you a sense of deep personal satisfaction? What is it about your work that you find most meaningful? Think of a time when you felt really inspired by your work – what were you doing? How were you thinking about your work?

Application
Look back at what gives meaning and purpose to your work.
- How can you avoid being sucked into 'being downcast'? What are the temptations to reflect on things that are deadening?

- What can you do to stay in touch with your hope, with the vision that gives life? Who can walk along the road with you?
- How can you make connections between your own concerns and the scriptures? How can you see your work as part of the work of the Church – the breaking of bread? How can you recognise Jesus walking with you on your journey?

 Reflection 2

The faith journey of the school
In the first reflection, you reflected on your own personal faith journey, and your own concerns. In this reflection, we reflect more on the role of faith development in the school, and the challenges that brings. We are exploring here the role of faith formation and development rather than simply information about religion.

- What are the concerns you see need to be clarified for people in the school? What are they talking about that makes them 'downcast'? What can be explained to them in terms of a wider vision to give them a sense that their deepest hopes are still alive? In what way can they be helped to see Jesus with them on their journey?

  Teachers   – older, experienced teachers?
                    – teachers in mid-career?
                    – beginning teachers?
  Students   – in senior cycle?
                    – new to the school, junior cycle?
  Parents   – in terms of their own children's development?
                    – in terms of their own personal growth?

- What are the structures which are meant to support and help people on their journey? How well are these supports working at the moment?
- Who are the main people in the school that provide the human accompaniment for others? Are there some people who do this as a formal role? Are there others who have an informal role? How are these people supported?

In promoting the faith journey and faith development within your school,
- What are your personal priorities?
- What would you like others in your school to have as priorities?
- What priorities might the Trustees have which would help you?

 ## THE TEMPTATIONS OF JESUS

Then Jesus was led by the Spirit out into the wilderness to be tempted by the devil. He fasted for forty days and forty nights, after which he was very hungry and the tempter came and said to him.

'If you are the Son of God, tell these stones to turn into loaves.'
But he replied, 'Scripture says:
Man does not live on bread alone,
But on every word that comes from the mouth of
God'.

The devil then took him to the holy city and made him stand on the parapet of the Temple.
'If you are the Son of God', he said,
'throw yourself down; for scripture says:

> *He will put you in his angels' charge,*
> *And they will support you on their hands*
> *In case you hurt your foot against a stone.*

Jesus said to him 'Scripture also says:
> *You must not put your God to the test.'*

Next, taking him to a very high mountain, the devil showed him all the kingdoms of the world and their splendour.
'I will give you all these' he said
'if you fall at my feet and worship me.'
Then Jesus replied
'Be off, Satan! For scripture says:
> *You must worship the Lord your God,*
> *And serve him alone'.*

Then the devil left him, and angels appeared and looked after him.

Matthew 4:1-11

 ## Reflection

This passage is set at the beginning of Jesus' ministry – his public life. The devil presents different options to him that focus on very different approaches to his ministry. In a way, this passage focuses on the dark side of leadership, on how leadership might go wrong.

Turning stones into bread
- If Jesus had given into this temptation, what would his ministry have been like? What miracles would he have worked? How would the people have reacted to him?

LEADING LIFE TO THE FULL

- How does this temptation apply to the work of a teacher or school leader? What expectations might people have of such a leader? How might a leader with this sense of mission act towards others?
- Providing bread from stones might seem like a good thing for others. Have you ever noticed ways in which apparently good things can be hidden temptations?

Demonstrating power
- If Jesus had given into this temptation, what would his ministry have been like? How would he have related to others, especially the poor in society? What response would he expect from others?
- What would this temptation look like to a teacher or school leader today? What type of power might they be tempted to show to others in the school community? What type of relationship might they look for with others?
- Power and expertise can be a good thing, when used properly. What is the key shift in this temptation to an improper use of power? Why did Jesus see this style of leadership as putting God to the test? How does this apply to us?

Accepting riches
- If Jesus had given into this temptation, what would his ministry have been like? What type of riches would he have accumulated? What demands might he have made on his followers?
- What type of riches might a teacher or school leader be tempted to acquire? What type of 'false god' or 'distraction' would this indicate? How would giving in to this temptation affect life in a classroom or school?
- Why did Jesus see the lure of riches as a temptation to worship a false god? What power do possessions and riches

have over our perspectives on life? How do you see this at work in yourself, in colleagues, in students and their families?

Application
- Which of these temptations are most common in your life?
- Has the pattern of temptation changed over time?
- How can you prepare yourself to recognise and respond to temptations to live a different kind of life than maybe you aspire to?

THEME 4

DEALING WITH OTHERS

Law and love

Our relationship with God is not a closed affair. It affects our attitudes and behaviour to other people. In the Old Testament, the precepts of the Law were quite detailed. In the New Testament, the precepts are less exact, but we are to be guided by the Spirit of love. In Matthew and Mark, Jesus was asked about the greatest of the commandments, and in Luke he was asked what must be done to inherit eternal life (Lk 10:25). He replied:

> You must love the Lord your God with all your heart, and with all your soul, and with all your mind. This is the greatest and the first commandment. The second resembles it: you must love your neighbour as yourself. On these two commandments hang the whole Law, and the Prophets also. (Mt 23:37-40)

In the Old Testament, the Law was closely connected with the covenant. It reflected man's obedient response to God's intervention in his life. The moral prescriptions were laid out in the Ten Commandments (Ex 20:1-17) and this was followed by a set of prescriptions covering the civil institutions of family, the economy and justice as well as instructions regarding rituals, ministry and cleanliness. The social structures of the Chosen People were embedded in a positive religious law. The Law became a symbol of the identity of Israel.

> See, as Yahweh my God has commanded me, I teach you the laws and customs that you are to observe in the land you are to enter and make your own. Keep them, observe them, and they will demonstrate to the peoples your wisdom and understanding. When they come to know of all these laws they will exclaim, 'No other people is as wise and prudent as this great nation'. And indeed, what great nation is there that has its gods so near as Yahweh our God is to us whenever we call to him? And what great nation is there that has laws and customs to match this whole Law that I put before you today. (Deut 4:5-8)

Jesus subjected himself to the Law. However, he also established a new covenant, stating that the Law and the Prophets were all pointing to John the Baptist. He had come not to abolish the Law, but to complete it (Mt 5:17). However, he approached the precepts of the Law from a fresh perspective. The new wine of the gospel was not to be poured into old skins (Mk 2:22). These new precepts set a higher standard than that of the old Law.

> If your virtue goes no deeper than that of the scribes and Pharisees, you will never get into the kingdom of heaven. (Mt 5:20)

> Go and learn the meaning of the words: *What I want is mercy, not sacrifice.* And indeed I did not come to call the virtuous, but sinners. (Mt 9:13)

Jesus set out challenges related to murder, adultery, divorce, taking oaths, seeking revenge and loving one's neighbour. He looked for a greater perfection where one did not get angry or call a brother names, look lustfully at another or swear in order to support one's word. Perfection required that one turn the other cheek and love one's enemy (Mt 5:21ff). He presented a sevenfold indictment of the scribes and Pharisees (Mt 23:13-26) who neglected the core message of the Law – discipleship, justice, mercy and honesty – and insisted on non-essential details. What Jesus objected to was not the Law itself, but an excessive formalism and casuistry that missed the core spirit of the Law, which is a faithful response to God. The focus on the Law carried with it the temptation to think that man could justify himself before God through his own obedience to the law, rather than seeing justice as based on God's grace and love.

For Paul, the key to salvation was the free gift of God in Jesus, rather than the Law. Whereas the Law and Prophets revealed God's justice to Israel, now that same justice was made known to Jew and pagan through the sacrifice of Jesus (Rom 3:21-24). This gift of love is 'poured into our hearts by the gift of the Holy Spirit' (Rom 5:5) which removes the need to be subject to the old Law. This was a point of much debate in the early church, especially when the pagans accepted the preaching of the apostles and came under pressure to submit to the full rigours of the Law and its rituals (Acts 10-11).

The law of love did not get rid of the old Law, but rather subsumed it. If one loved God properly, one still followed the law of God. In John's gospel, there is a change of terminology. The *Law* refers to the old formalism of the Jewish Law. He prefers the term *Commandment* for the new dispensation. Jesus has received his command from the Father:

> What I had to speak was commanded by the
> Father who sent me, and I know that his

commands mean eternal life. And therefore what
the Father has told me is what I speak.
(Jn 12:49-50)

Discipleship is linked with keeping the commandment of love.
It contains both the promise of God's love and the human
response to this love.

> If anyone loves me he will keep my word and my
> Father will love him, and we shall come to him and
> make our home with him. (Jn 14:23)

> Whatever we ask him, we shall receive, because
> we keep his commandments and live the kind of
> life that he wants. His commandments are these:
> that we believe in the name of his Son Jesus Christ
> and that we love one another as he told us to.
> Whoever keeps his commandments lives in God
> and God lives in him. (1Jn 3:22-24)

The key insight is the unity between loving God and loving
one's neighbour. Just as Jesus consistently pointed out the
hypocrisy of scribes and Pharisees in placing the burden of the
Law on others and then not following it themselves, the
apostles preached the importance of understanding the new
community that exists because Jesus redeemed all people,
making us all brothers and children of God (1 Jn 3:1-2). This
brings with it obligations on how we behave towards others.

> My children, our love is not to be just words or
> mere talk, but something real and active; only by
> this can we be certain that we are children of the
> truth. (1 Jn 3:18-19)

Anyone who says, 'I love God', and hates his brother, is a liar, since a man who does not love the brother that he can see cannot love God, whom he has never seen. So this is the commandment that he has given us, that anyone who loves God must also love his brother. (1 Jn 4:20-21)

This love is not simply a philanthropic concern for those less well off than oneself, a sharing of one's abundance. Many of the parables of Jesus indicate the type of love we can have for our neighbour – the Good Samaritan (Lk 10), the father of the Prodigal (Lk 15) and the owner of the vineyard (Mt 20) all went beyond the call of justice to help their neighbour. Jesus commends the widow who put in two coins to the offering.

I tell you truly, this poor widow has put in more than any of them; for these have all contributed money they had over, but she from the little she had has put in all she had to live on. (Lk 21:3-4)

At the final judgement, we will be told that when we welcomed the poor and comforted them, we welcomed Jesus himself, and we will be rewarded with eternal life.

This love is not an aimless charity, something we perform for our own good. It is genuine empathy with those who are poor or troubled. The care we show to others is motivated by a vision of God's care. This is not blind to the reality of sin or deviance. As well as caring for others, there are many examples in the gospels where Jesus confronted and even condemned others for their attitudes. He warned Chorazin, Bethsaida and Caparnaum that they were in danger of suffering a worse fate than Tyre, Sidon and Sodom because they did not appreciate the miracles that were worked for them. He castigated the scribes and Pharisees in very strong language, calling them hypocrites and whitewashed tombs (Mt 23) for their behaviour. In anger, he threw the money changers out of the temple. Jesus was always clear that there were consequences for sin, and this was usually expressed as eternal fire.

Jesus worked from a clear vision of what was good. He was not afraid to confront others who did not live according to these principles. But he also described how one should settle disputes. First the two parties in dispute should try and solve the problem. If that does not work, they you take one or two others along as witnesses. If that fails, the dispute goes to the community. If one party does not accept the wisdom of the community then they are to be 'treated like a pagan or a tax collector' (Mt 18:20).

The problem therefore is not the existence of the Law, but rather the way we use it. If we depend on it to secure order and right living, as if we can do everything from our own resources, then we are doomed to failure. The love that we have for one another is the work of God in us. It comes from our experience of being forgiven in our own lives by God. It is a gift from God and signifies our union with Him. According to John, Jesus prayed at the Last Supper:

> I have made your name known to them and will continue to make it known, so that the love with which you loved me may be in them, and so that I may be in them. (Jn 17:26)

Christians love because they have experienced God's love in their own lives. Their love is an imitation of this divine love and this imitation is the witness we give to God's love for us.

Try, then to imitate God, as children of his that he loves, and follow Christ by love as he loved you.
(Eph 5:1-2)

I give you a new commandment: love one another; just as I have loved you, you also must love one another. By this love you have for one another, everyone will know that you are my disciples.
(Jn 13:34-35)

In schools, there can often be a tension between the commands of the Law and the commandment of love. We express this as a tension between a rigid discipline code and the pastoral care element of the school. Anywhere there are large numbers of young people, you need rules and regulations to ensure smooth running, to train students to respect other people's rights and to protect the common good. At the same time, many young people need help in coping with both the social and academic demands of schools. For some young people, the school is the only place they may find peace and acceptance in an otherwise turbulent life. For others, the constraints of school life may be quite oppressive. The key for the school is to find a balance between 'the Law' that helps people to live and work together, and a pastoral care system that reaches out to all those who need help.

The first two passages for this theme consider the generosity of response in the Good Samaritan and the father of the Prodigal. The third passage reflects on the existence of weeds among the good seed and how we might respond to that. The last two passages look at how we view wrong-doing. The passage from Matthew 12 looks at behaviour being a manifestation of internal character, and the final reflection looks at two passages where Jesus confronts sinners.

THE GOOD SAMARITAN

The man was anxious to justify himself, and said to Jesus

'And who is my neighbour?"

Jesus replied

'A man was once on his way down from Jerusalem to Jericho and fell into the hands of brigands: they took all he had, beat him and then made off, leaving him half dead.

Now a priest happened to be travelling down the same road, but when he saw the man, he passed by on the other side.

In the same way, a Levite who came to the place saw him, and passed by on the other side.

But a Samaritan traveller who came upon him was moved with compassion when he saw him.

He went up and bandaged his wounds, pouring oil and wine on them.

He then lifted him on to his own mount, carried him to the inn and looked after him.

Next day, he took out two denarii and handed them to the innkeeper.
'Look after him,' he said 'and on my way back I will make good any extra expense you have'.

Which of these three, do you think, proved himself a neighbour to the man who fell into the brigands' hands?

'The one who took pity on him' he replied.

Jesus said to him 'Go, and do the same yourself.'

Luke 10:29-37

 Reflection

Think of the two men who passed by the robbed man.
- What do you imagine they talked about when they got to their business in Jerusalem – the lack of policing on the road – the need for a better medical service?
- What was the difference between them and the Samaritan? Do you think they were really unconcerned, or just frightened to be involved, or did they think the man lying on the road was drunk or something else?
- What types of excuses would be used to pass by someone like that to-day?

Think of the Samaritan.
- What impressed you most about the reaction and the behaviour of the Samaritan?
- Suppose the Samaritan had arrived a little earlier. What do you think he would have done? How could he have been a good neighbour to the robbers?
- What in the Samaritan's behaviour do you think Jesus wants us to imitate as Christians?

Give an example of people in schools today who fit into the following roles in the parable. What attitudes do they portray?
- the robbers
- the man beaten up
- the priest and Levite
- the Samaritan
- the innkeeper
- How is God neighbour to each of these groups ?
- Who are you in this parable? Who plays the other roles?
- How does God show himself as neighbour to you?
- What evidence do you have of people in the school playing the role of the Good Samaritan?
- How well do we appreciate these people?
- How well does the victim appreciate the Good Samaritan?
- How can we move beyond the human experience to understand God at work in this experience? (i.e. move from solidarity to transcendence.)

 ## THE PRODIGAL SON

When he was still a long way off, his father saw him and was moved with pity. He ran to the boy, clasped him in his arms and kissed him tenderly. Then his son said 'Father, I have sinned against heaven and against you. I no longer deserve to be called your son.' But the father said to his servants, 'Quick! Bring out the best robe and put it on him; put a ring on his finger and sandals on his feet. Bring the calf we have been fattening, and kill it; we are going to have a feast, a celebration, because this son of mine was dead and has come back to life; he was lost and is found.' And they began to celebrate.

Now the elder son was out in the fields and on his way back, as he drew near the house, he could hear music and dancing. Calling one of the servants, he asked what it was all about. 'Your brother has come,' replied the servant, 'and your father has killed the calf we had fattened because he has got him back safe and sound.' He was angry then and refused to go in, and his father came out to plead with him; but he answered his father, 'Look, all these years I have slaved for you and never once disobeyed your orders, yet you never offered me so much as a kid for me to celebrate with my friends. But, for this son of yours, when he comes back after swallowing up your property – he and his women – you kill the calf that we had been fattening.'

The father said 'My son, you are with me always and all I have is yours. But it was only right we should celebrate and rejoice, because your brother here was dead and has come to life; he was lost and is found.'

Luke 15:18-32

 Reflection

The scene recounts how the Prodigal son returned to his father.
- What experiences are there in schools of people trying to turn over a new leaf, or take on new behaviour? How easy is it for leaders, teachers or students to change in the school?
- If someone wanted to change, who would be the 'father figure' in this parable? How would he be seen to be waiting? How would he welcome the person, and the change? What would the celebration feast look like?

- Who is the 'elder brother' figure among the teachers and among the students? Do they have real reason to be jealous or angry about how others are treated in the school? How do they express this?
- What is the response of those who are 'forgiven', or 'treated lightly'? How common is this attitude? In what way does it affect morale?
- How does the experience of forgiveness affect morale in the school
  - among students?
  - among staff?
  - among parents?
- In what way can a school celebrate both kinds of 'sons', both among the staff and among the students?
- As a teacher or as a leader, what role do you identify with most in the parable? Is there any role you would like to explore more?

 ## THE PARABLE OF THE DARNEL

The kingdom of heaven may be compared to a man who sowed good seed in his field. While everybody was asleep his enemy came, sowed darnel all among the wheat, and made off. When the new wheat sprouted and ripened, the darnel appeared as well.

The owner's servants went to him and said, 'Sir, was it not good seed that you sowed in your field?

If so, where does the darnel come from?'

'Some enemy has done this' he answered.

And the servants said,
'Do you want us to go and weed it out?'

But he said,
'No, because when you weed out the darnel you
might pull up the wheat with it.
Let them both grow till the harvest;
and at harvest time I shall say to the reapers;
First collect the darnel and tie it in bundles to be
burnt,
then gather the wheat into my barn.'

Matthew 13:24-30

An explanation of this parable is given in Matt 13:36-43

 Reflection

- What do we see as 'good seed' and what do we classify as 'darnel'?
- How does the 'good seed' and the 'darnel' appear, growing side-by-side in:
  - the school?
  - the classroom?
  - individual students?
  - individual teachers?
  - individual leaders?
- Who is seen as 'the enemy' that brings the darnel?
- What is the temptation to 'weed it out'? How does this present itself in any (or all) of the scenarios above?
- What is the danger of trying to weed out the darnel in these scenarios?

- In what way does the good seed get separated from the darnel over time?
- What are the benefits and challenges of allowing the good seed and the darnel to grow together?
- How have you experienced God allowing this to happen in your own life?
- How to you grow in accepting good seed and darnel in your own life? In the lives of others?

 ## CHARACTER COMES FROM WITHIN

Make a tree sound and its fruit will be sound;
Make a tree rotten and its fruit will be rotten.
For the tree can be told by its fruit.

Brood of vipers!
How can your speech be good when you are evil?
For a man's words flow out of what fills his heart.
A good man draws good things from his store of goodness;
a bad man draws bad things from his store of badness.

So I tell you this,
that for every unfounded word men utter
they will answer on Judgement day,
since it is by your words you will be acquitted,
and by your words, condemned.

Matthew 12:33-37

A parallel version of this passage can be found in Luke 6:43-45

LEADING LIFE TO THE FULL

- What are the key images that stay with you from this passage? How do you respond to the tone of the passage?
- If we try to apply the image 'a tree can be told by its fruit' to the school context, what types of fruit do we expect to find among:
  - leaders?
  - teachers?
  - pupils?
  - parents?
- Are there any dangers in classifying people as 'good' or 'bad' according to this type of fruit? What other explanations might exist for 'good' or 'bad' fruit?
- In your experience of dealing with others, how consistent are people in drawing from their 'store of goodness' and their 'store of badness'? What challenges does this pose to you in developing attitudes towards these people and in dealing with their behaviour?
- Are there ways in a school that classifications of 'good' and 'bad' trees can be institutionalised? What are these structures in relation to pupils? In relation to teachers? In relation to parents?
- The last paragraph challenges us to live authentic lives? What are the types of words that will lead to us being 'acquitted'? When do we get the opportunity to practice these words?
- Where are the greatest dangers for inauthenticity? In what type of situation might our words lead to condemnation?
- How do we maintain a reflective practice on our own words, and our attitudes to others? What encouragement do we need? How can we encourage others?

DISCIPLINE AND CONFRONTATION

1 Woman caught in adultery

The scribes and Pharisees brought a woman along who had been caught committing adultery; and making her stand there in full view of everybody, they said to Jesus, 'Master, this woman was caught in the very act of committing adultery, and Moses has ordered us in the Law to condemn women like this to death by stoning. What have you to say?' They asked him this as a test, looking for something to use against him.

But Jesus bent down and started writing on the ground with his finger. As they persisted with their question, he looked up and said 'If there is one of you who has not sinned, let him be the first to throw a stone at her.' Then he bent down and wrote on the ground again.

When they heard this they went away one by one, beginning with the eldest, until Jesus was left alone with the woman, who remained standing there. He looked up and said, 'Woman, where are they? Has no one condemned you?'
'No one, sir,' she replied.
'Neither do I condemn you,' said Jesus, 'go away, and don't sin any more'.

John 8:2-11

2. Jesus clears the temple

Jesus went into the Temple and began driving out those who were selling. 'According to scripture,' he said, 'my house will be a house of prayer. But you have turned it into a robbers' den'.

Luke 19:45-48

 Reflection

These two passages contrast different ways Jesus dealt with people who had broken the rules.

- In reflecting on the rules that were broken, which do you think was most serious – adultery or selling in the temple? Why?
- Why do you think Jesus treated the people involved differently?
- In the first passage, why do you think the people moved away, one by one? What is the significance of the older ones going first? What did the people learn from the experience?
- What might bystanders have learnt from the experience of watching Jesus driving out the money-changers?
- What did the people who were dealt with learn from the experience – the woman and the money-changers?
- Who do the different characters stand for in a school situation;
  - the woman caught in adultery?
  - the money-changers?
  - the crowd looking for justice?
  - the onlookers in the Temple?
  - Jesus?

- In reflecting on these passages, what does Jesus teach us about the importance of rules, and dealing with those who break rules? How can this be applied in a school situation – with teachers and with students?

THEME 5

TEACHING

The role of teaching

The story of the scriptures is basically a story of education – the education of the chosen people and of the early Church. God is the supreme teacher, leading the people by precept and by trials to obedience to the Law or obedience in faith. As a teacher, God reveals, exhorts, promises, chastises, rewards and gives an example to the people. Most of the teaching is done through the prophets, who transmit a knowledge of divine things and the practical consequences of that knowledge.

Teaching in the Old Testament

The family is the first source of teaching. In the covenant attached to the Exodus and the Passover, the family ritual is clearly the first source whereby children learn the significance of their history and the key events that are celebrated.

> Let these words of mine be written in your heart and in your soul; fasten them on your hand as a sign and on your forehead as a circlet. Teach them to your children and say them over to them, whether at rest in your house or walking abroad, at your lying down or at your rising. Write them on the doorposts of your house and on your gates,

so that you and your children may live long in the land that Yahweh swore to your father he would give them for as long as there is a sky above the earth. (Deut 11:18-21)

Moses was the first teacher in a formal sense, as he brought the covenant to the people (Deut 24:3). The priests continued this teaching in the temple, especially on the major feast days. The teaching consisted mainly of promulgation, explanation and exhortation.

> Moses committed this Law to writing and gave it to the priests, the sons of Levi, who carried the ark of Yahweh's covenant, and to all the elders of Israel. And Moses gave them this command: 'At the end of every seven years, at the time fixed for the year of remission, at the feast of Tabernacles, when the whole of Israel come to look on the face of Yahweh your God in the place he chooses, you must proclaim this Law in the hearing of all Israel. Call the people together, men, women, children and the stranger who lives with you, for them to hear it and learn to fear Yahweh your God and keep and observe all the worlds of this Law.
> (Deut 31:9-12)

The prophets also played a role as teachers. They received their message directly from God, rather than teaching the 'prescribed text' of the Law. However, they were disciples of the Law, and their preaching assumed that the Law was known. Mainly, they exhorted people to follow the Law.

Despite all the teachers around them, the belief in the Old Testament is that God is the teacher. This is part of the prayer life of the people.

LEADING LIFE TO THE FULL

Yahweh is so good, so upright,
He teaches the way to sinners;
In all that is right, he guides the humble,
And instructs the poor in his way. (Ps 25:9)

However, the people did not always listen to their teachers. Hence, God punished this unfaithful people in order to rid them of their hardness of heart. However, the prophets promised that Yahweh would eventually reveal himself as the true teacher of Israel, and those who accepted his teaching would live in happiness and prosperity.

> When the Lord has given you the bread of suffering and the water of distress, he who is your teacher will hide no longer, and you will see your teacher with your own eyes. (Isa 30:20)

> Your sons will all be taught by Yahweh. The prosperity of your sons will be great. You will be founded on integrity. (Isa 54:13)

This promise was fulfilled in the New Testament with the coming of Jesus.

Jesus as teacher

The public ministry of Jesus is essentially a ministry of teaching. Luke describes the start of the ministry:

> When he started to teach, Jesus was about thirty years old. (Lk 3:23)

When arrested in the garden, Matthew tells us:

> It was at this time that Jesus said to the crowds,
> 'Am I a brigand, that you had to set out to capture
> me with swords and clubs? I sat teaching in the
> Temple day after day, and you never laid hands on
> me.' (Mt 26:54)

Jesus taught in formal situations, such as when he visited the synagogues and in the temple. When he returned to Nazareth, he was invited to read from the scroll and speak to the congregation. He also taught on informal occasions, on a mountain, or from a boat, or in the countryside. He gave extra tuition to his disciples away from the crowds.

Jesus was recognised as a good teacher by those around him. In Luke's gospel, we are told that even at the age of twelve, the elders in the temple were astounded at his intelligence (Luke 2:47). At the beginning of his ministry, the people in his home town 'were astonished at the gracious words that come from his lips' (Lk 4:22). When he taught in Capernaum, on a Sabbath, 'his teaching made a deep impression on them because he spoke with authority' (Lk 4:31). He had this authority because the message he taught was given him by his Father (Jn 8:28). Jesus was given the title 'Rabbi' by the learned men he met although he was clear that this is not a title to be sought by his disciples.

> You, however, must not allow yourselves to be
> called Rabbi, since you have only one Master, and
> you are all brothers. You must call no one on earth
> your father, since you have only one Father, and he
> is in heaven. Nor must you allow yourselves to be
> called teachers, for you have only one Teacher, the
> Christ. (Mt 23:8-10)

LEADING LIFE TO THE FULL

The next theme looks in more detail at Jesus as a role model for teachers.

Teaching and the early church

Before the ascension, Jesus gave his disciples the mission to 'Go, make disciples of all the nations ... teaching them to observe everything that I have commanded you' (Mt 28:19). This mission was given in the context of the promise of the Holy Spirit, the Spirit of truth, leading humankind to the very fullness of truth (Jn 16:13), teaching them to understand the mystery of Christ – how he fulfils the scriptures, the meaning of his words, his actions and signs – all of which have remained hidden until now.

> I have said these things to you while still with you; but the Advocate, the Holy Spirit, whom the Father will send in my name, will teach you everything and remind you of all I have said to you. (Jn 14:25-26)

The apostles testify that at the time they did not understand the significance of events, but after the resurrection, they remembered what had been done (Jn 2:22). Their own enlightenment was a key element of their teaching. Like Jesus, the apostles taught in the synagogues, in the temple and in private homes. At first, they were very successful and impressed many with the authority of their message. However, their early success was linked with a gift of tongues that enabled each person to hear them and understand them in their own language.

As the early church grew in numbers, the apostles travelled throughout the empire spreading the good news. They taught in the local synagogues, and also in the market place. As well as teaching and preaching, a number of other 'charisms' developed to support the work of the Church. Also, there was a growing body of doctrine. The scriptures were written down, and in cases of dispute, issues were sent back to Jerusalem so that the apostles could decide on the appropriate response. A key concern for the apostles was to protect the young church from the erroneous doctrines of false teachers.

> The time is sure to come when, far from being content with sound teaching, people will be avid for the latest novelty and collect themselves a whole series of teachers according to their own tastes; and then, instead of listening to the truth, they will turn to myths. (2 Tim 4:3-4)

From a very early stage in the Church, the purpose of teaching and preaching the good news was clear. However, there were different approaches to teaching, depending on the audience. It is worthwhile examining some of these approaches.

Styles of teaching

In the early church, there seemed to be three main approaches to teaching. The first of these was called *kerygma*. This amounts to a proclamation of the message of salvation. This was how the apostles first proclaimed that Jesus was the Messiah. Their kerygma consisted of three basic messages:

1 The apostles were witnesses to Jesus' death, resurrection and ascension into heaven.
2 Jesus' ministry was heralded by John the Baptist, inaugurated by teaching and miracle, completed by the appearances of the risen Christ and by the gift of the Holy Spirit.

3 Jesus fulfils the prophecies of the Old Testament, and therefore begins the messianic era. They invited Jews and pagans to repentance so that Jesus' glorious return may come soon. (Acts 2:14-39; 3:12-26; 4:8-12; 5:29-32; 10:34-43 and 13:16-41)

The second form of teaching is called preaching. Just as the priests of the Old Testament instructed the people in the meaning of the Law, so also the apostles instructed the people by reinterpreting the scriptures for them in the light of the resurrection. Thus, preaching was a form of instruction. It is worth noting that some of these 'classes' were not always models of good practice. For instance, despite Paul's greatness, he was a very wordy preacher, and sometimes did not hold the attention of his audience.

> On the first day of the week we met to break bread. Paul was due to leave the next day, and he preached a sermon that went on till the middle of the night. A number of lamps were lit in the upstairs room where we were assembled, and as Paul went on and on, a young man called Eutychus who was sitting on the window-sill grew drowsy and was overcome by sleep and fell to the ground three floors below. He was picked up dead. Paul went down and stooped to clasp the boy to him. 'There is no need to worry,' he said 'there is still life in him.' Then he went back upstairs where he broke bread and ate and carried on talking till he left at daybreak. They took the boy away alive, and were greatly encouraged. (Acts 20:7-12)

So, perhaps there is hope for all of us as teachers!

A third form of teaching was the parable. This was used mainly by Jesus, but no doubt the parables were repeated by the pastors in the early Church. The parable was a story that pointed to key elements of Jesus' message – the love of God, moral responsibilities to our neighbour, an invitation to the kingdom. Frequently, Jesus used contrasts and apparent contradictions (the role of the Samaritan, or the sinner) to arouse curiosity and encourage further reflection. The images used in the stories related to the culture and life of the people.

A key element of all teaching is to relate the message to the people being taught. There is a sense of a growing community in the New Testament. First, the people heard the message. Then they were sustained in that message. But there is also a sense of the sacredness of the message itself, and the need to respect it. For Matthew, all sacred things are to be held in great respect.

> Do not give dogs what is holy; and do not throw
> your pearls in front of pigs, or they may trample
> them and then turn on you and tear you to pieces.
> (Mt 7:6)

In other words, sacred teaching of great worth, like the consecrated meat of the temple, must not be set before those who can not receive it with profit and may even abuse it. This too forms part of the challenge of teaching.

Images applied to teaching today

In reflecting on our own role as educators, it seems worthwhile to reflect on different types of teaching. As in the Old Testament, a special place is given to the family. It provides a basic teaching and establishes a support for a child's learning. We have seen in the theme of leadership style how the teaching functions of priest, king and prophet can be embedded in the school. Each of these roles teaches in a different way. As with Jesus' teaching, the modern teacher is expected to recognise formal and informal opportunities to promote learning. There is always the demand for 'large group' teaching, where the material has widespread distribution to all in the class. There is also the need for individual and small group attention, where material is adapted or linked to personal experiences.

The experience of the early Church was a tension between a living, charismatic approach to the message and delivering a formal doctrine. Teachers in schools today often experience a similar tension between developing a love of learning by free exploration of a subject, and the need to cover a fixed syllabus. This tension seems to be a universal challenge.

The kerygmatic approach in the early Church responded to the charismatic aspect of the message. It forced listeners to reflect on their need for salvation and then pointed them to the source of that salvation in Jesus. The work of motivating students and catching their attention is a modern form of kerygma. Preaching is related to direct instruction. Teachers help students to explore their subject areas. They explain patterns, rules and procedures within the subject and help the student appreciate the different nuances. A key function of the leadership role is to help participants to understand the mission and values of the organisation. At times this requires direct teaching, as for example, explaining the need for a particular policy statement.

The focus on parables reflects a modern approach to active learning. We recognise more and more the need to engage the student in the material to be learnt. We talk about the importance of relevance, and in the case of organisational learning, we realise that teachers must take ownership of the school values. Teachers and leaders are involved in constructing dramatic illustrations or parables to help students and colleagues reflect on their current values and lead them to deeper experiences of these values.

In this section we present three reflections. The first passage is taken from Paul's Second Letter to Timothy, and deals with the concern for content. In the main it explores the role of king and priest in teaching. The other two passages, one from the Old Testament and the second from the new, reflect more on the prophetic role in teaching. The different seasons and the different soils for sowing seeds look at what is an appropriate education for different groups, and also how is the best way to approach that education.

 ## SOUND DOCTRINE

Before God and before Christ Jesus who is to be judge of the living and the dead, I put this duty to you, in the name of his Appearing and of his kingdom:

Proclaim the message and,
 welcome or unwelcome,
 insist on it.
Refute falsehood,
 correct error,
 call to obedience.
Do all with patience, and with the intention of teaching.

The time is sure to come when, far from being content with sound teaching, people will be avid for the latest novelty and collect themselves a whole series of teachers according to their own tastes; and then, instead of listening to the truth, they will turn to myths.

Be careful always to choose the right course; be brave under trials; make the preaching of the Good News your life's work, in thoroughgoing service.

2 Timothy 4:1-5

 Reflection

- In what way do you experience teaching or leadership in education as:
  - proclaiming the Good News?
  - refuting falsehood?
  - correcting error?
- How does this manifest itself:
  - in a directly religious context?
  - in the day-to-day events of the classroom or the school?
- What do you see as the sources of falsehood and error for students and teachers?
  - What makes it so attractive for people to turn away from sound teaching?
  - What are the myths that they embrace?
  - What are the signs of a 'false doctrine' of 'myth'?
- What alternatives are offered by the Gospel message?
  - What is it that makes this unattractive to people?
  - How might people recognise 'meaning' and 'true value'?

- As you reflect on your own life, what can you do to maintain a focus on 'sound doctrine' and making life-giving choices?
- In your work with others, what attracts them to reflect on a deeper level on the consequences of their choices and the nature of 'sound doctrine'?
- What can be done to help young people or colleagues reflect on and share their experience of meaning in their lives?
- How are they supported, and how can they be supported in the future, in being faithful to this call?

 ## SEASONS IN EDUCATION

There is a season for everything, a time for every occupation under heaven:

A time for giving birth, a time for dying;
A time for planting, a time for uprooting what has been planted.

A time for killing, a time for healing;
A time for knocking down, a time for building.

A time for tears, a time for laughter;
A time for mourning, a time for dancing.

A time for throwing stones away, a time for gathering them up;
A time for embracing, a time to refrain from embracing.

A time for searching, a time for losing;
A time for keeping, a time for throwing away.

A time for tearing, a time for sewing;
A time for keeping silent, a time for speaking.

A time for loving, a time for hating;
A time for war, a time for peace.

What does a man gain for the efforts that he makes?

I contemplate the task that God gives mankind to labour at. All that he does is apt for its time; but though he has permitted man to consider time in its wholeness, man cannot comprehend the work of God from beginning to end.

I know there is no happiness for man except in pleasure and enjoyment while he lives.
And when man eats and drinks and finds happiness in his work, this is a gift from God.

Ecclesiastes 3:1-11

 Reflection

The writer presents life as a series of contradictory acts – some leading to happiness, others to sorrow.

- As you read through the different sets of activities, what strikes you as important? How do you recognise the pattern in your own life? What has the balance been? For example, in what way have you noticed 'giving birth' or 'planting"; 'dying' or 'uprooting' in your own life? Has there been more 'planting' than 'uprooting'? Has the balance changed at different times in your life?

- What would you hope to achieve in each of the different sets? What do you think are the opportunities and challenges for you?
- Read the sets again, this time reflecting on the students in your class, or the teachers in the school. What might these phrases mean for them at this stage?

Among students:
  - What is being planted or uprooted?
  - How are they searching for, or loving?
  - What are they loving or hating?
  - How do you respond to their activities?
  - How do you see your role in helping them in achieving a balance?

Among teachers:
  - Do you see teachers at different stages with these activities?
  - How do you read the balance of these activities in the school?
  - How does the staff cope with 'tears and mourning'?
  - How do they celebrate 'laughter and dancing'?

- What can be done to help people at an individual level?
- How can the community of the school come to a better understanding of a Christian balance of these activities?

As you 'contemplate the tasks' of education:
- Can you see this work as a 'gift from God'?
- What aspects of the work are blocks to experiencing God's presence?
- What aspects of the work give you a particularly deep sense of God's presence?
- How do you repond to that gift?

Imagine a sower going out to sow. As he sowed, some seeds fell on the edge of the path, and the birds came and ate them up. Others fell on patches of rock where they found little soil and sprang up straight away, because there was no depth of earth; but as soon as the sun came up they were scorched and, not having any roots, they withered away. Others fell among thorns, and the thorns grew up and choked them. Others fell on rich soil and produced their crop, some a hundredfold, some sixty, some thirty. Listen, anyone who has ears.

Matthew 13:4-9

The Parable Explained

When anyone hears the word of the kingdom without understanding, the evil one comes and carries off what was sown in his heart; this is the man who received the seed on the edge of the path. The one who received it on patches of rock is the man who hears the world and welcomes it at once with joy. But he has no root in him; he does not last. Let some trial come or some persecution on account of the word, and he falls away at once. The one who received the seed in thorns is the man who hears the word, but the worries of this world and the lure of riches choke the word and so he produces nothing. And the one who received the seed in rich soil is the man who hears the word and understands it; he is the one who yields a harvest and produces now a hundredfold, now sixty, now thirty.

Matthew 13:18-23

 Reflection

- Imagine yourself as the sower. What are the seeds you sow as a leader or teacher?
- What do the three images:
  - the edge of the path;
  - the patches of rock;
  - the thorny ground;

  stand for in your work? How does this compare to the rich soil?
- In what ways do the images of poor ground signify the failure of the seeds you sow as a leader or teacher to grow to full maturity? How do you react to each of these situations or types of people? How does it affect you?
- What does a 'good harvest' look like to a teacher or school leader? How do you recognise this? How do you celebrate it?
- As a teacher or leader, what responsibility do you have for preparing the seed for planting?
- What responsibility do you have for preparing the ground?
- How do you prepare the different types of ground mentioned in the parable?

JESUS AS THE MODEL TEACHER

In the last theme we saw how the story of the scriptures was the story of God teaching his people. Jesus, as the Son of God, is the perfect example of this teaching. Not only is Jesus the teacher, but he is also the message. In John's gospel we are told that:

> The Word was made flesh, he lived among us, and
> we saw his glory, the glory that is his as the only
> Son of the Father, full of grace and trust. (Jn 1:14)

Therefore, in reflecting on Jesus as the model teacher, we look not only at what and how he taught, but also at who he was.

If we are to follow Jesus in being good teachers, we can be like Thomas and doubt Jesus, and doubt our own understanding of the message. However, when Thomas raised his doubts to Jesus, Jesus told him:

> I am the Way, the Truth and the Life. No one can
> come to the Father except through me. If you know
> me, you know my Father too. From this moment,
> you know him and have seen him. (Jn 14:6-7)

This quotation in some way outlines a programme for the teaching career, for it tells us how Jesus understood himself as a model for us. In it, we see three elements of the curriculum, and also three ways of being with those who are learning.

Jesus as the Way

When John the Baptist proclaimed the coming of Jesus, he proclaimed a baptism of repentance for the forgiveness of sins and quoted Isaiah 'Prepare a way for the Lord' (Lk 4:3-4). Jesus, the new Messiah, was to the new Moses, a guide, an escort and a leader.

In the Old Testament, the way of the Lord was seen in external terms – it was made up of the Law and the history of salvation. The Chosen People sought to live according to this way, because it led to life. The prophets frequently called them back to this way, and to repent of the evil ways they had embraced.

> Let the wicked man abandon his way, the evil man
> his thoughts. Let him turn back to Yahweh who
> will take pity on him, to our God who is rich in
> forgiving; for my thoughts are not your thoughts,
> my ways not your ways – it is Yahweh who speaks.
> (Is 56:7-8)

Jesus also taught people the way to the Father. His way brought the Law to perfection, and proclaimed the new law of love. As a teacher, he was the Light of the World, showing others the path. At the Transfiguration, he gave his chosen disciples a foretaste of the heavenly kingdom, but also pointed out to them that the way included the cross. He travelled the road to Jerusalem and his own sacrifice. He did so in obedience to the Father, thus marking out the way for us. His sacrifice gained access for us to the Kingdom:

> In other words, brothers, through the blood of
> Jesus we have the right to enter the sanctuary, by a
> new way which he has opened for us, a living

opening through the curtain, that is to say, his body. (Heb 10:19-20)

Jesus also called his disciples to follow him. His followers were to live the same life as he did, and carry out the same work. In describing his relationship with his followers, Jesus spoke of himself as the Good Shepherd.

> The one who enters through the gate is the shepherd of the flock; the gatekeeper lets him in, the sheep hear his voice, one by one he calls his own sheep and leads them out. When he has brought out his flock, he goes ahead of them and the sheep follow because they know his voice. (Jn 10:2-4)

In explaining this parable to the disciples, Jesus also claimed to be the gate of the sheepfold (Jn 10:7), as well as having all the characteristics of the good shepherd, who is prepared to lay down his life for the sheep.

The way is no longer the law, but a person. Instead of following a set of 'dead' commandments, we follow a living person.

> You must live your whole life according to the Christ you have received – Jesus the Lord; you must be rooted in him and built on him and held firm by the faith you have been taught, and full of thanksgiving. (Col 2:6-7)

> Try then to imitate God, as children of his that he loves, and follow Christ by loving as he loved you, giving himself up in our place. (Eph 5:1-2)

Indeed, the members of the early church were known as followers of the Way. (cf. Acts 9:2)

As teachers, we also share in the mission of teaching the way of the Lord, and showing that to others. We also show them the way by our own example of being followers ourselves.

Jesus as the Truth

The dictionary definition of truth is:

> Faithfulness; constancy; veracity; agreement with reality; fact of being true; actuality; accuracy of adjustment or conformity; the true state of things, the facts; a true statement; an established fact. (*Chambers*)

In the Bible, truth is more related to religious experience than to judgments. To walk in the truth is to have a deep sense of communion with God that comes from following his Law. Thus, truth and wisdom are closely linked. In the New Testament, believers are described as those who have accepted the word of truth, and who live in obedience to that truth.

> It is not because you do not know the truth that I am writing to you but rather because you know it already and know that no lie can come from the truth. The man who denies that Jesus is the Christ, – he is the liar, he is the Antichrist; and he is denying the Father as well as the Son. (1Jn 2:21-22)

To live in the truth is to live in light. Otherwise, we live in darkness. The key to the truth is to admit our own sin, and to seek conversion.

> If we say we have no sin in us, we are deceiving ourselves and refusing to admit the truth; but if we acknowledge our sins, then God, who is

faithful and just, will forgive our sins and purify us from everything that is wrong. (1 Jn 1:8-9)

Jesus himself prayed that his disciples would remain faithful to the truth of the word he had shared with them.

> Holy Father, keep those you have given me true to your name, so that they may be one like us. While I was with them, I kept those you had given me true to your name. (Jn 17:11-12)

> Consecrate them in the truth; your word is truth. As you sent me into the world, I have sent them into the world, and for their sake I consecrate myself so that they too may be consecrated in truth. (Jn 17:17-19)

At his trial before Pilate, he testified on his own behalf:

> Yes, I am a king. I was born for this, I came into the world for this; to bear witness to the truth; and all who are on the side of truth listen to my voice' 'Truth? Said Pilate 'What is that?' (Jn 18:37-38)

For John, Jesus is the revelation of truth. His truth is linked with grace, which is a sign of our reconciliation with God.

> Though the Law was given through Moses, grace and truth have come through Jesus Christ.
> (Jn 1:17)

For Jesus, the words he preaches are the truth. Accepting them allows his hearers to live in the truth of God's love and become his disciples.

To the Jews who believed in him Jesus said: 'If you make my word your home you will indeed be my disciples, you will learn the truth and the truth will make you free. (Jn 8:31-32)

He was also convinced of the truth to which he witnessed. He was the way to salvation, through the words he spoke. He challenged those who did not believe in him, or his words:

If I speak the truth, why do you not believe me? A child of God listens to the words of God; if you refuse to listen, it is because you are not God's children. (Jn 8:46-47)

At the ascension, he promised to send the Holy Spirit, also the Spirit of Truth, to be with them at all times.

I have said these things to you while still with you; but the Advocate, the Holy Spirit, whom the Father will send in my name, will teach you everything and remind you of all I have said to you. (Jn 14:25-26)

The apostles in the early church were conscious that they were inviting followers to the same truth that Jesus preached. They did not preach an abstract doctrine.

For Christ did not send me to baptise, but to preach the Good News, and not to preach that in the terms of philosophy in which the crucifixion of Christ cannot be expressed. The language of the cross may be illogical to those who are on the way to salvation, but those of us who are on the way see it as God's power to save. (1Cor 1:17-18)

As the early Church grew, so also the preaching became more formalised. The gospels were written down, and there was a concern among the apostles that the different communities would adhere to the true teaching of the apostles.

> Brothers, I want to remind you of the gospel I preached to you, the gospel that you received and in which you are firmly established; because the gospel will save you only if you keep believing exactly what I preached to you – believing anything else will not lead to anything. (1Cor 15:1-2)

There was a growing concern about the number of false teachers who were coming into the communities. In particular, Paul warns the different communities about the effects of listening to teaching that does not lead to the truth.

> As I asked you when I was leaving for Macedonia, please stay at Ephesus, to insist that certain people stop teaching strange doctrines and taking notice of myths and endless genealogies; these things are only likely to raise irrelevant doubts instead of furthering the designs of God which are revealed in faith. The only purpose of this instruction is that there should be love, coming out of a pure heart, a clear conscience and a sincere faith. There are some people who have gone off the straight course and taken a road that leads to empty speculation; they claim to be doctors of the Law, but they understand neither the arguments they are using nor the opinions they are upholding. (1Tim 1:3-7)

Teaching therefore leads people to the truth. It leads them to a deep experience of God in their lives. This experience comes not just through understanding facts about creation, but in the experience of a communion with Jesus, as he leads creation to its final destiny. This experience, this 'living the truth', involves a deep sense of being at peace with God's love and call.

Jesus as Life

Jesus claims that he came so that we may have life, and have it to the full (John 10:10). His ministry included healing people and raising the dead to life, symbolic actions proclaiming his power over life and over sin, which destroys life. In his preaching, he constantly points people to life, and encourages them not to be distracted by empty riches, but rather to store up riches in heaven, where real life is.

> That is why I am telling you not to worry about your life and what you are to eat, nor about your body and how you are to clothe it. Surely life means more than food, and the body more than clothing! (Mt 6:25)

Jesus focused on eternal life. He told the Samaritan woman at the well that he would give living water.

> Anyone who drinks the water that I shall give will never be thirsty again: the water that I shall give will turn into a spring inside him, welling up to eternal life. (Jn 4:14)

In the Eucharistic discourse, he tells his disciples about the life he offers them.

I am the bread of life. He who comes to me will
never be hungry; he who believes in me will never
thirst. (Jn 6:35)

After forgiving the woman caught in adultery, Jesus spoke
about the life that comes from living in faith:

I am the light of the world; anyone who follows
me will not be walking in the dark; he will have the
light of life. (Jn 8:12)

After raising Lazarus from the dead, Jesus points to an even
greater gift of life.

I am the resurrection. If anyone believes in me,
even though he dies, he will live, and whoever lives
and believes in me will never die. (Jn 11:25-26)

Jesus also laid down his life for us, as the good shepherd, so that
he could reclaim his life and share it more abundantly with us.
At baptism, the Christian enters into a new life with God. Paul
tells us we are baptised into his death, and we rise with him.
Our new relationship with God is a share in his divine life. We
become heirs rather than servants of the kingdom. Our lives
are a thanksgiving and a celebration of this gift.

When John begins his epistle, he writes that Jesus not only
tells us about eternal life, but he also was that life made
visible.

Something which has existed since the beginning,
that we have heard and we have seen with our own
eyes; that we have watched and touched with our
hands; the Word, who is life – this is our subject.
That life was made visible; we saw it and we are

giving our testimony, telling you of the eternal life which was with the Father and has been made visible to us. What we have seen and heard we are telling you so that you too may be in union with us, as we are in union with the Father and with his Son Jesus Christ. We are writing this to you to make your own joy complete. (1 Jn 1:1-4)

This too is one of the aims of education. It helps people to find life. The hope of any education system is that people come to appreciate the world they live in and the opportunities open to them. They come to understand at a deeper level who they are and the gifts they have. They develop skills in using these gifts. Education helps people to discover their own potential, the hope that lies within them, and to pursue that vision. It is the commitment to pursuing this vision that leads us to the fullness of life. A Catholic education does not change the world we live in, or the life we face. The Christian is not immune from the joys and sorrows of life. Rather our Catholic education transforms the way we live our lives. It is in the meaning we give to events that we find that transformation.

 LORD, TEACH US TO PRAY

Now, once he was in a certain place praying, and when he had finished, one of his disciples said, 'Lord, teach us to pray, just as John taught his disciples'.

He said to them, 'Say this when you pray; Father, may your name be held holy,

Your kingdom come,
Give us each day our daily bread,
And forgive us our sins,
For we ourselves forgive each one who is in debt to us,
And do not put us to the test.'

He also said to them,

Suppose one of you has a friend and goes to him in the middle of the night to say,

'My friend, lend me three loaves, because a friend of mine on his travels has just arrived at my house and I have nothing to offer him'.

And the man answers from inside the house,

'Do not bother me. The door is bolted now, and my children and I are in bed. I cannot get up to give it to you.'

I tell you, if the man does not get up and give it to him for friendship's sake, persistence will be enough to make him get up and give his friend all he wants.

So I say to you;
Ask, and it will be given to you;
search and you will find;
knock, and the door will be opened to you.
For the one who asks always receives;
the one who searches always finds;
the one who knocks will always have the door opened to him.
What father among you would
hand his son a stone when he asked for bread?
Or hand him a snake instead of a fish?
Or hand him a scorpion if he asked for an egg?

If you then, who are evil, know how to give your
children what is good,
how much more will the heavenly Father give the
Holy Spirit to those who ask him!

Luke 11:1-12

Reflection

- Why did the disciples want to learn to pray?
- What was it about the disciples of John the Baptist that attracted them or inspired them?
- How might this apply in the school community?
- Does anyone inspire you to pray?
- Might your life inspire anyone else to pray?
- What does Jesus teach us about God in the Our Father?
- How do you think these lessons apply in a school community?
- Can you give examples of where they are evident?
- Can you give examples of where they are not practised?
- How can this prayer be made more personal for you? For your school community?

Take the example Jesus gave of perseverance in prayer.
- What do you pray for?
    - your colleagues?
    - your students?
    - their parents and families?
    - why might these groups of people be frustrated with their prayer?
    - what hope does this story offer each of these groups?
    - how can this hope be mediated to them?

- What is the point of Jesus' image of 'ask and you shall receive'?
  - How does this work in practice?
  - What attitudes do we need to bring to prayer when we are asking for things?
  - How have you been helped to develop these attitudes?
  - How can you help others develop these attitudes?

 ## JESUS TEACHES IN PARABLES

The reason I talk to them in parables is that they look without seeing and listen without hearing or understanding. So, in their case this prophecy of Isaiah is being fulfilled;

You will listen and listen again, but not understand,
See and see again, but not perceive.

For the heart of this nation has grown coarse,
their ears are dull of hearing,
and they have shut their eyes for fear
they should see with their eyes,
hear with their ears,
understand with their heart,
and be converted,
and be healed by me.

But happy are your eyes because they see,
your ears because they hear!

I tell you solemnly,
many prophets and holy men longed to see what
you see, and never saw it;
to hear what you hear, and never heard it.

Matt 13:13-17

Reflection

- According to Jesus, what is the point of a parable?
- Where does he expect people to find the parables from which they can learn?
- What 'parables' have you learnt from in your life?
- Have other people shared their parables with you?
- Are you ever inspired by other people's stories, or their lives?
- What in life makes our hearts coarse, our ears dull and our eyes shut?
- What can we do to remain open to God's parables in our lives?
- Who does school help achieve this openness:
  - teachers?
  - students?
  - parents?
- In what way can people fear learning from parables?
- In what way can they be surprised and happy?

LEADING LIFE TO THE FULL

THERE IS ONLY
ONE TEACHER

Addressing the people and his disciples, Jesus said, 'The scribes and the Pharisees occupy the chair of Moses. You must therefore do what they tell you and listen to what they say; but do not be guided by what they do, since they do not practise what they preach. They tie up heavy burdens and lay them on men's shoulders, but will they lift a finger to move them? Not they! Everything they do is done to attract attention, like wearing broader phylacteries and longer tassels, like wanting to take the place of honour at banquets and the front seats in the synagogues, being greeted obsequiously in the market squares and having people calling them Rabbi.

You, however, must not allow yourselves to be called Rabbi, since you have only one Master, and you are all brothers. You must call no one on earth your father, since you have only one Father, and he is in heaven. Nor must you allow yourselves to be called teachers, for you have only one Teacher, the Christ. The greatest among you must be your servant. Anyone who exalts himself will be humbled, and anyone who humbles himself will be exalted.

Matthew 23:1-12

- The opening verses give a strong condemnation of the hypocrisy of the scribes and Pharisees. How might this be applied to teachers or school leaders?
- What are the key areas of school life that act as traps for teachers or leaders where they might fall between what they 'preach' and what they 'practise'?
  - In their relationship with colleagues?
  - In their relationships with students?
- What attitudes and practices need to be cultivated so as not to fall into these traps?
- How do you see Jesus cultivate these attitudes and practices in his life?
- What supports you in trying to imitate Jesus as a teaching role model?